THE POCKET GUIDE TO
freshwater
fish
OF BRITAIN AND EUROPE

First published in 2001 by
Mitchell Beazley, an imprint of
Octopus Publishing Group Ltd
2–4 Heron Quays,
London E14 4JP

This edition published in 2010 by Bounty Books,
a division of Octopus Publishing Group Ltd
2–4 Heron Quays, London E14 4JP

www.octopusbooks.co.uk

An Hachette UK Company
www.hachette.co.uk

Executive Editor   Vivien Antwi
Executive Art Editor   Kenny Grant
Project Editors Chloë Garrow, Michelle Bernard
Art Editor   Christine Keilty
Designer   Peter Gerrish
Production   Jessame Emms
Fish illustrations   Stuart Carter
Habitat illustrations   Rudi Vizi
Photography   Malcolm Greenhalgh

ISBN 978-0-753719-55-8

Printed and bound in China by Toppan Printing Company Ltd

Bounty
Books

THE POCKET GUIDE TO

freshwater
fish

OF BRITAIN AND EUROPE

MALCOLM GREENHALGH

Illustrations by STUART CARTER

Contents

Introduction 6

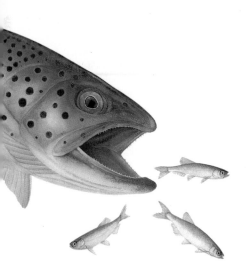

Introduction

This book is a pocket guide that can be used to identify the fish species that might be encountered in European freshwater habitats.

Having spent many years with rod and line catching fish, in 1986 I began an intensive study of European freshwater fish: their identification, growth, populations, how they bred, what they ate and other aspects of their behaviour. This involved much travel with rods and lines, pond net, bottle-traps, binoculars and polarising sunglasses: it is surprising how much you can see of fish behaviour if you sit down quietly by a clear stream or pool and simply watch!

It is also surprising what a home-made minnow-trap will reveal, or a few minutes of grabbing about amongst weed or boulders with a simple pond net. Watching anglers have looked on in amazement at the populations of fish species they had never imagined were living in *their* water, where *they* fished: brook lampreys, loaches, and perhaps huge numbers of miller's thumbs. My obsession also involved a search of the literature as well as discussion with other anglers and students of fish behaviour.

Many observations were first published in magazines and journals. Then my observations on trout were published in 1989 in *The Wild Trout* (with Rod Sutterby) and on salmon in 1996 in *The Life of the Salmon* (Vol I in *The Complete Salmon Fisher* series). The distillation of all my fish observations was finally published in 1999 in *Freshwater Fish*, published by Mitchell Beazley.

Freshwater Fish not only describes every species of European freshwater fish, but it includes a detailed summary of the breeding behaviour and life cycle, foods and feeding behaviour, longevity and growth, distribution and habitats of most species. Notes are also given on the populations and conservation status of every species: most anglers and naturalists are unaware that over a quarter of Europe's freshwater fish are endangered!

Freshwater Fish is a fairly large textbook, and quite unsuitable for use in the field. So it was pleasing when Mitchell Beazley approached me with the idea of producing an accompanying pocket guide that could slip into the pocket and be used to identify fish at the waterside. Unfortunately space does not allow the behaviour of the fish to be described here. Nor does it allow for the identification of very local or minor species, or species of doubtful validity (see p 7). These can, however, all be found in the larger *Freshwater Fish* which you can keep at home for reference on your return from the field.

MALCOLM GREENHALGH

Fish species

In the 19th century naturalists split many species into a host of so-called separate species. For instance, in 1886 H G Seeley split what we today call the brown trout into 26 separate European species. Through the first half of the 20th century 'splitters' went out of fashion and 'clumpers' appeared on the scene. They demanded good, solid scientific grounds before they would accept the splitting of species into two or more. What to the splitter was considered enough to identify one fish population as a species – colour differences and perhaps a slight difference in the shape of a fin or the number of spines or rays in a fin – to the clumper was simply natural variation within one species. So by the 1960s there was a fairly well accepted minimalist list of Europe's freshwater fish.

Then, towards the end of the 20th century, splitting came back in fashion, triggered mainly by a drive to reassess and bring about some change, not for the simple sake of change but to justify the cost of the research! So, for example, in 1886 Seeley described six 'species' of Balkan dace: *Leuciscus svallise*, *L. illyricus*, *L. ukliva*, *L. polylepis*, *L. turskyi* and *L. microlepis* solely on grounds of differences in lateral line scale counts. When I began my researches they had all been clumped in to the one species *L. svallise* (see p 86-7), but in recent years attempts have been made to resurrect the 1886 split!

This is, I believe, wrong. Messing about with species names may be intellectually satisfying and provide some academic kudos to those who play the game. Yet for those of us naturalists who need good established species names for practical purposes, the splitting trend – that is happening in most groups of plants and animals as well as fish – does wildlife a great disservice.

This pocket guide gives a practical treatment of European fish species; the larger textbook *Freshwater Fish* outlines some of the problems of species definition.

Why European freshwater fish have such strange distributions

The River Danube has 79 species of native fish but Iceland has only six. France and Germany have 53 and 59 native species respectively, but southeast England only 42 and Scotland 17. Why?

At the height of the last great Ice Age, that began to retreat from Europe about 15,000 years ago, most of the continent was covered in snow and ice, or was colder than today with long icy winters. Most of today's lakes and rivers were then fishless, with the fish populations being centred on five main refuges: in Iberia, in the Rhône valley in S France, in the Po valley of N Italy that also included the dried-up Adriatic Sea, in NW Greece and in the Danube and other rivers around the Black Sea.

As the ice melted, leaving behind liquid lakes and rivers, so they became hospitable to fish provided the fish could reach them, for (with the exception of the eel, p 42-3) fish cannot cross dry land.

Some fish can live in sea water: lampreys, eel, salmon, brown trout, arctic charr, whitefish, smelt, sticklebacks, sea bass, mullets, blenny and gobies. They were able to enter the ice-free rivers and colonise them and any lakes in the river system. They would not be able to pass high waterfalls, so that many high-level mountain lakes and streams could not be colonised.

Other species that cannot tolerate saltwater could colonise only by swimming through freshwater rivers and lakes. At the end of the great melt, about 10,000 years ago, there was far more freshwater habitat than there is today. Sea level was also lower and regions now separated by the sea were linked by dry land and freshwater lakes and rivers: e.g. SE Britain to the River Rhine, Sweden and Finland to Germany and Poland. So fish spread from the refuges and, where there was a freshwater connection, colonised.

Fish species that survived in the Iberian refuge were blocked from passing into France and further east by the Pyrenean mountain chain through which there was no freshwater passage. Thus we find some species (e.g. Escalo and calandino roaches, p 95, and Iberian and Portuguese

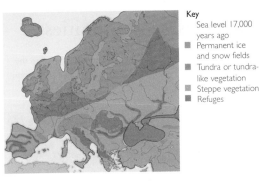

Europe at maximum glaciation about 17,000 years ago. Much of the continent was in the grip of snow and ice and the freshwater fish restricted to Ice Age refuges. It was in these refuges that many of the fish species and subspecies we see today evolved, and from these refuges that fish colonised the rest of Europe after the last Ice Age ended.

Key

Sea level 17,000 years ago

■ Permanent ice and snow fields

■ Tundra or tundra-like vegetation

Steppe vegetation

■ Refuges

barbels, p 121) trapped in Iberia. Also few, if any, purely freshwater fish could cross from France to Iberia.

Similarly, several species passed from Germany to SE Britain before the English Channel was formed, and from Germany and Poland to Finland and Sweden before the Baltic flooded. But these same species (roach, chub, bream, pike etc.) were unable to pass on to NW Britain and Ireland, to Iceland or to NW Norway because there was no freshwater route through. And some species were too late to pass before the seas inundated the freshwater route. Thus the ide, moderlieschen, bitterling, asp and nase are native to one side of the Channel in France, Belgium, Holland and Germany, but not England.

Through the last millennium the natural distribution has been influenced greatly by man. European fish have been transported to areas they never reached naturally. Carp to western Europe, pike and perch to NW Britain and Ireland, and trout from lowland rivers and lakes to mountain tarns. Rainbow trout and speckled charr are just two species brought from North America. These transportations were of food fish. More recent ones, of cyprinids to Ireland and barbel to rivers where they are not native, were for angling purposes.

Such introductions continue to be made. Today the Asiatic grass carp (*Ctenopharyngodon idella*) is raised in fish farms and released to lakes and rivers to control weed. But it cannot breed in European waters.

River fish communities

Most rivers rise high in mountains and flow down to the sea. As they do so, their character changes and so do their fish communities.

High mountain stream water turbulent and bed unstable boulders; water with few plant nutrients; few water plants.

Trout zone Brown trout dominant, with grayling, eel, immature salmon and minnows in the fish community.

Upper river water less turbulent; bed stable gravel in meander bend pools but less stable boulders in riffles. Increasing nutrients; some water plants.

Grayling zone Grayling dominant, with brown trout, eel, immature salmon, minnows, nase, chub, dace, miller's thumb, stone loach and brook lamprey in the fish community.

Middle river water less turbulent; bed stable sand or silt or fine gravel in meander pools and stable gravel with boulders in riffles. Increasing nutrients. Increasing water plants.

Barbel and Chub zone Barbel and chub dominant with some brown trout and grayling, minnows, nase, dace, pike, eel, loach and lampreys.

Lower river water lacks turbulence; bed stable silt or compacted gravel; increasing nutrients; lush weed growth.

Bream zone Bream and other cyprinids (eg roach and dace) dominant, with pike, perch, eels and zander. Salmon and sea trout may pass through.

Estuary

The river meets the sea through its estuary. Some freshwater species may feed in the estuary (e.g. trout, zahrte and zeige); some marine species may ascend high in the estuary (mullet, bass and flounder), and other species pass to and fro through the estuary as they move between feeding and spawning areas (sea lamprey, shads and salmon).

Lake fish communities

Lakes vary in size from small ponds to vast inland seas, and in depth from shallow reedy meres to valley lakes over 100m in depth. However, the principles of lake natural history are common to all.

1 The more plant nutrients the more plant growth; plant growth includes weeds rooted on the bottom and planktonic algae drifting in the open water.
2 The more planktonic algal growth the less far light can penetrate through the water.
3 Plants need light to grow, so the more planktonic algae, the less deep light penetration and the shallower the zone in which rooted plants can grow.
4 The more plant growth the more invertebrates and the more food for fish.
5 With few exceptions (eg char in oligotrophic lakes) most fish are found in lake shallows.

Oligotrophic lake
This extreme type of lake has a rock bed, few nutrients, sparse vegetation, great light penetration, and small fish populations. Such lakes are found in mountainous regions with few human habitations and little agriculture. With such little plant life there are only meagre populations of plant-eating invertebrates (such as mayflies), resulting in tiny populations of slow-growing fish. Trout and arctic charr or whitefish dominant, with minnows and eels.

Eutrophic lake
This other extreme type of lake usually has a mud, silt or sand bed, high nutrient levels, luxuriant plant growth, very shallow light zone, and huge fish populations. The richest eutrophic lakes are found in lowland regions and are usually surrounded by intensively farmed land and are close to towns and cities. Cyprinids dominant, with eels, pike, perch, zander, catfish and sticklebacks.

There is also a middle range of lake productivity, the mesotrophic lake. Such lakes are found in lowlands where the agriculture is not intensive and where there are no large towns and cities. They can support the widest range of lake fish species. Because of the greater productivity than oligotrophic lakes, brown trout grow rapidly; but because these lakes are less productive than eutrophic lakes, cyprinids tend to grow more slowly.

All types of lake can be enriched through an increase in the human population in the catchment and through the introduction of more intensive agriculture adding nutrients to the water. During the twentieth century, some oligotrophic lakes became mesotrophic, and some mesotrophic lakes becamse eutrophic. As a result, many fish communities were altered.

Oligotrophic lake
This type of lake typically has a rocky bed, sparse vegetation, great light penetration and small fish populations.

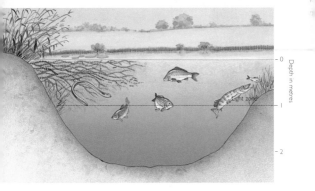

Eutrophic lake
These lakes have a sand or mud bed, luxuriant plant life, a very shallow light zone and a huge fish population.

Canal and drain fish communities

Canals are man-made waterways, originally designed to transport ships and barges but often today increasingly used for leisure (angling, boating and walking). Drains are deep drainage channels cut through low-lying country to turn marshland into farmland.

Canals usually have a shallow margin on at least one side, but with drop-offs to the deep boat channel. The shallows are usually richly vegetated, with weedbeds extending to the deep channel which is usually kept clear of weed by dredging.

Drains are usually kept clear of weed, and have no extensive shallow margins.

Because canals and drains tend to occur in lowland areas with rich countryside around, the water tends to

have lots of plant nutrients and these produce lush weed and plankton growths. Invertebrate populations are large and include plankton, such as Daphnia and Cyclops, as well as larger species, such as hog-lice, water-boatmen and dragonfly nymphs. These are all fish-foods and may generate large populations of fast-growing fish.

The fish species occurring in canals depends largely on what was introduced into the waterways once they were built, although some fish may have colonised from inflowing streams. Cyprinids are usually dominant, especially popular anglers' species such as roach, rudd, bream, tench and carp. Pike and perch are usually common, sometimes with zander. In recent years increasing numbers of aquarium species have been released to canals: goldfish and members of the American sunfish family (pumpkinseed and black and brown bullheads). Eels usually find their own way to canals and drains.

Canals
Canals are often linear aquatic wildlife corridors, carrying water, plants, insects, molluscs and amphibians, as well as fish, into European cities and intensely farmed areas. Canals are also the last refuge for aquatic wildlife species in the many lowland fens, lakes and meres that have been drained in the last 250 years. Beds of reed, rush and sedge harbour isolated populations of reed warblers and sedge warblers. Coot and moorhens feed on the open water, and in the spring frogs, toads and newts return to the canal to spawn. There is more to the canal than water and fish!

Conservation problems

On 30 January 2000, 95 million litres of water containing
a high concentration of cyanide leaked into the River Tisa
from a gold mine close to the town of Baia-Mare,
Romania. By 13 February the poison had passed
downstream through Hungary and on into the Danube
close to the Bosnian capital Belgrade. By that time it had
wreaked destruction on most Tisa wildlife, including its
entire fish stocks. In just the length of the Tisa flowing
through Hungary, 83 tonnes of dead fish were removed
from the river by clean-up teams, and of fish-eating birds,
white-tailed eagle and herons had been found dead.
An early estimate indicated that it would take the
Tisa and the Danube below the confluence at least ten
years to recover.

One report (*Daily Telegraph*, 15 February 2000) quoted
the Australian mining company Esmerelda Exploration
as saying that: 'the facts of the incident had been grossly
exaggerated', that 'freak weather caused the initial
overflow', and that 'the overflow from a dam at the
Baia Mare mine could not have caused fish deaths many
miles downstream.'

The Danube system has 79 native species of fish, of
which 15 are special to the Danube and adjacent rivers.

Such pollution 'accidents', which are invariably the
result of negligence, are all too common today in a Europe
where economic progress is considered, by governments
and industry, to be far more important than environmental
issues. If recent trends are to continue, between these
words being written and this book being published, at
least two more major river pollution 'incidents' will have
occurred somewhere in Europe.

However, major catastrophic incidents are only one
side of pollution.

Long-term industrial and sewage effluent pollution
Industrial towns produce wastes, including sewage from
their human inhabitants. Traditionally towns, which were
often built by rivers and often just upstream of the estuary,
used the river as a drain for this effluent. Into the river;
out to sea; gone from mind!

Through the 19th and 20th centuries most of the major
western European rivers suffered from this on-going
pollution: notably the Thames, Tees, Mersey, and the

Rhine. The effects of this pollution were to destroy any fish living at and below the source of pollution, and to prevent fish that pass through estuaries (salmon, sea trout, shads, sturgeon and eels) from using the entire river. Thus were salmon virtually exterminated from most rivers flowing into the English Channel, North Sea, S Baltic from Brest in NW France to the Gulf of Finland, and from the Thames, Mersey and Tees. The collapse of NW European shad populations was entirely due to estuary pollution.

Fortunately improvement in effluent treatment has slowly begun to clear this long-term pollution in many rivers, so that by the beginning of the third millennium, salmon were again running the Thames, Tees and Rhine.... but not yet the Mersey.

The cleaning up of long-term, low-level pollution has had an interesting effect on some rivers. Low level organic pollution increases productivity in rivers. Invertebrate populations increase and they feed an increased fish – usually cyprinid – population. From the 1950s to the mid-1980s two English rivers (the Trent and Ribble) were famous for the large bags of fish caught by anglers; 30-50kg catches of chub, roach and other species were not uncommon. The cleaning-up resulted in a great reduction of natural foods in these rivers and made big catches a thing of the past. That these rivers still held smaller stocks of cyprinids as well as increasing populations of clean-water species such as trout, salmon and grayling was little compensation for the big-bag-seeking bait-fishers!

Fertiliser pollution

The European Union subsidises fertilisers containing high concentrations of nitrogen, phosphorus and potassium (N, P, K). So NPK fertilisers are scattered on fields bordering rivers and lakes, and a high proportion reaches the water. The effect, in hot, bright, sunny weather, is to generate massive growths of the blanket-weed alga *Cladophora*.

Cladophora chokes the river and lake bed, killing invertebrates (and fish eggs) that need a high oxygen level. It prevents the growth of water weeds that are beneficial to the river or lake (e.g. water buttercup *Ranunculus*). And it encourages the concretion of gravel and boulders in the river bed.

The European taxpayer's money is spent by the EU to pollute rivers and lakes unnecessarily.

Acidification

Power stations in England, Poland and Germany produce nitric and sulphuric acids that are jettisoned into the atmosphere through tall chimneys. These gases come back to earth as 'acid rain' and pollute rivers and lakes in areas of high rainfall: western and northern Britain, and S Scandinavia. In the second half of the 20th century, some lakes and rivers were rendered fishless, or had their fish stocks drastically reduced, through acid rain.

'Scrubbers' can be fitted to power stations to reduce acid gas release, but this is often deemed 'too expensive'.

Pesticide pollution

Farm organo-halide pesticides were responsible for the decline of many wildlife species in the second half of the 20th century. These are now banned through most of Europe. However, the recent development of pyrethroid dip pesticides to combat sheep parasites has destroyed the insect populations of many river stretches and threatened fish populations.

River damming

Many species of fish can survive in rivers only if they can freely pass up and down the stream. Damming, installed mainly for hydroelectricity generation, has resulted in a collapse of some fish species even in cases where the dam has a built-in fish pass.

Alien fish species

The introduction of alien species is always a threat to native ones. The introduction of American mosquito fish, for instance, has contributed to the decline of the Spanish toothcarp (p 154), and the introduction of ruffe (168) into two British lakes is threatening the survival of the lakes' whitefish populations. The introduction of non-native fish into any water should be considered a form of pollution.

Drainage

The drainage of coastal wetlands along the Mediterranean coast is threatening the toothcarps, and many populations of tiny, small-water species such as swamp minnows, mudminnows and nine-spined stickleback have been lost through the drainage of 'waste' wetland.

The drainage of damp pastures and meadows, and marshy uplands (to make the land 'more productive'), results in more violent river spates following rain and, during long droughts, the falling of river levels to dangerous levels. Some rivers have dried up during droughts and their fish stocks lost.

Water abstraction

The abstraction of water – whether from bore holes tapping underground aquifers or by the damming of headwater streams – has resulted in low river floes and levels, reducing fish stocks. In some instances, entire rivers have dried up permanently.

Ignorance

Unfortunately the European media and the public (including many conservationists) care little for aquatic wildlife other than appealing mammals such as otters and seals and spectacular birds such as ospreys, kingfishers and herons. The result of this is that few are aware of the critical state of European fish stocks. Of the 174 fish species now living in Britain and Europe, 22 are introduced and 152 native. And of the native species, at least 42 are endangered.

This small chalk-stream once held brown trout, minnows, stone loach and lesser numbers of roach, chub and pick. Overabstraction took away the water… the fish… and the stream is now no more.

Identifying fish

Whilst many species of fish can be identified by a glance (eg pike and tench), other closely related species may involve a closer examination. When examining a specimen and using descriptions given later in this guide (which are based on labelled illustrations) you may have to pick out certain structures on the fish. The labelled illustration below shows the main structures.

Colour Can vary greatly within some species. But some coloured markings are useful in making identifications (eg lower fins in charrs).

Rays and spines Fins are supported by branched segmented rays and by spines. The number of spines in a fin is given in Roman numerals, branched spines in Arabic.

Fin positions These can be useful in separating closely related species (eg in the Mediterranean barbel the front of the base of the dorsal fin is slightly in front of the base of the pelvic fins, whereas in the barbel the two are in line).

Shape of fin-free edge This may be straight, concave or convex.

Mouth and jaw Does the tip of the snout extend beyond the lower jaw, or the lower jaw extend further than the snout? Is the mouth 'underslung'? Does the rear of the jaw extend to or beyond the rear of the eyes? Is the snout pointed or blunt?

Scale counts The lateral line count is the number of scales along the lateral line. In salmonids, the adipose count is the number of scales from the adipose fin to the lateral line.

Gills To confirm the identification of some species it is useful to examine the gill rakers that are on the inside of the gill arch (gill filaments on the outside of the arch). *See also* Glossary p 188.

Shown here Humpback salmon

Snout

Nostril

Mouth

Snout length

Eye diameter

Eye

Jaws

Head length

Gill cover

Head

Lateral line

Pectoral fins

Belly

Sides

Overall length

Dorsal fin

Vent

Pelvic (ventral) fins

Back

Anal fin

Adipose fin

Tail length

Tail

Tail (caudal) fin

Max. body depth

Using pharyngeal teeth for identifying cyprinids

Extract pharyngeal teeth

Kill the fish quickly and take it home. You can store it in a deep-freeze, but do not put it in pickling solution as this can erode the pharyngeal teeth.

1. Carefully remove the gill cover without damaging gills.
2. Remove each gill by severing the gill arches at the bottom and top.
3. The slender pharyngeal bones (one to either side of the throat) are now exposed. Remove these carefully by severing the bones at the top and bottom.
4. Drop the bones/teeth into hot water and leave them there to soak for several minutes; then clean and remove the soft tissues gently using a fine brush.
5. Record the teeth as:
x1+y1+z1 : z2+y2+x2
x = number in outer row,
y = number in middle row,
z = number in inner row
(assuming there are 3 rows),
1 = the right-hand side pharyngeal teeth, 2 = the left-hand side pharyngeal teeth. Check both sides as in some species the number, usually in the first row, may be different.
6. Examine the teeth with a lens. Are the teeth hooked at the tip? Have they flat grinding edges? Have they ridge-like serrations? Compare your findings to this table.

Common name
Three rows of pharyngeal teeth
carp
barbel
Two rows of pharyngeal teeth
silver bream
schneider
bleak
asp
gudgeon
white-finned gudgeon
grass carp
dace
Balkan dace
ide
chub
soufie
zeige
minnow
swamp minnow
rudd
One row of pharyngeal teeth
crucian carp
gibel/goldfish
tench
bream
Danube bream
blue bream
zahrte
nase
southwest European nase
minnow nase
moderlieschen
bitterling
roach
escalo roach
Danube roach

Pharyngeal teeth no.	Pharyngeal teeth description
3+1+1 : 1+1+3	flattened surface
5+3+2 : 2+3+5	pointed with hooked tips
5+2 : 2+5	flattened with weak hook
4 (or 5)+2 : 2+4 (or 5)	slender with slight serrations at tip
5+2 : 2+5	serrated close to tip and hooked
5+3 : 3+5	smooth, with slight hook
5+3 (or 2) : 2 (or 3)+5	pointed with weak hooks
5+3 : 3+5	pointed and slightly hooked
2+4 (or 5) : 4 (or 5)+2	flattened, with folded sides and groove on grinding surface
5+2 (rarely 3) : 2 (rarely 3)+5	smooth with hooked tips
5+2 : 2+5	slender and smooth
5+3 : 3+5	smooth, pointed; may have slight hook at tip
5+2 : 2+5	smooth or weakly serrated, hooked tip
4 (or 5)+2 : 2+4 (or 5)	very slender, slight serrations
5+2 : 2+5	slender, slight hook at tip
5+2 : 2+5	very slender
5+2 : 2+5	very slender and fragile
5+3 : 3+5	with ridge-like serrations
4 : 4	smooth, flattened tips
4 : 4	smooth, slender
4 (or 5) : 4 (or 5)	tips often broader than base
5 : 5	flattened along sides
5 : 5	flattened
5 : 5	flattened
5 : 5	flattened and knife-like
6 : 6	narrow and dagger-like
5 : 5	flattened and knife-like
5 : 5	slender and slightly flattened
4 (or 5) : 4 (or 5)	very fine
5 : 5	very fine
usually 5 : 5 (occasionally 6)	variable; some may be hooked or have a ridge running down the length
5 : 5	slender and slightly flattened
5 : 5	slender and slightly flattened

Sea Lamprey *Petromyzon marinus*

The sea lamprey is the largest of the European lampreys, eel-like fish that lack gill covers and have a sucker disk instead of a jawed mouth. Sea lampreys are most often found dead or dying after returning from the sea and spawning.

Distribution Kola Peninsula and southern Iceland, south and west (including British Isles) to southern Spain, and east to Italy.

Habitat Clean rivers (where estuary pollution and dams do not prevent access).

Feeding Attaches to host fish with sucker and digests host's flesh.

Size Most 50-60cm in length, 2kg weight; exceptionally to 1m.

Distinct notch separating rear dorsal fin from tail fin

First of two clearly separated dorsal fins

Rear dorsal fin larger than front dorsal fin and tail fin

No scales and no paired fins

Seven breathing holes on each side of the body

Heavy black or dark brown mottling on back

Sucker disc with one tooth-plate having 7-9 pointed cusps, lots of small teeth and large teeth in front of the mouth

Light olive-brown body and paler belly when fish is at sea

Lampern (River Lamprey) *Lampetra fluviatilis*

Eel-like, but lacking gill covers and paired fins, and with a sucker disc instead of jaws, the lampern spawns in rivers and goes to sea to feed and grow. Most usually found dead, in late spring or summer, after spawning.

Distribution British Isles (except far north), southern Fenno-Scandia and Baltic States, and most of western Europe east to Slovenia and N Italy.

Habitat Clean undammed streams where the estuary is clean enough for the fish to pass through.

Feeding Attach to host fish with sucker disc and digest tissues and blood of host.

Size Average about 30cm long, 60g in weight.

Other similar species Siberian lamprey (*L. japonica*) occurs from Kola Peninsula eastwards.

All fins are brown

Rear of two well-separated dorsal fins

Scaleless, smooth skin

Uniform olive- or grey-brown above, shading to golden-olive or yellow on sides and white belly

Sucker disc with two tooth-plates, front with two blunt cusps, rear with 7-10 pointed cusps; few small teeth.

Golden iris with brown fleckings

Line of seven breathing holes along each side

Brook Lamprey *Lampetra planeri*

As in all lampreys, lacks gill covers and paired fins and, instead of a jawed mouth, has a sucker disc. This smallest European lamprey does not migrate to sea, nor does it feed on other fish. Nocturnal, and most often found buried in silt or fine gravel.

Distribution British Isles, and southern Fenno-Scandia and the Baltic States south to northern Italy, east to the Black Sea and west to the Pyrenees.

Habitat Clean rivers and small streams.

Feeding Immature brook lampreys feed by straining bacteria, algae and detritus from the water and mud. Adults do not feed.

Size Usually in the range 10-15cm in length.

Other similar species Zanandrea's lamprey (*L. zanandreai*) occurs in rivers draining in to the north of the Adriatic Sea.

Rear dorsal fin is larger than the front dorsal fin

Dull yellow sides

Sucker disc with two tooth-plates, front lacking cusps, rear with 6-9 blunt cusps; few blunt teeth.

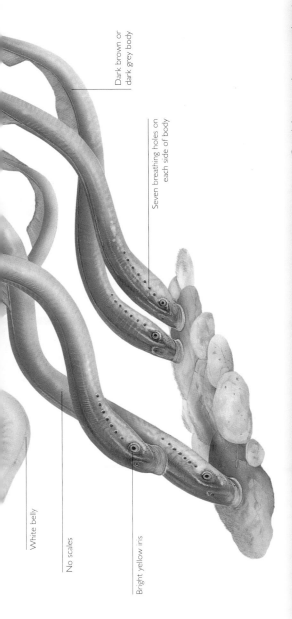

Dark brown or dark grey body

Seven breathing holes on each side of body

White belly

No scales

Bright yellow iris

Danubian Lamprey *Eudontomyzon danfordi*

A typical lamprey, eel-like but lacking paired fins, and with a sucker disc instead of jaws and with breathing holes instead of gill covers, the Danubian lamprey lives all its life in freshwater. They are most often found in shallow feeder streams, dead after spawning.

Other similar species *E. vladykovi* (S. Danube system), *E. mariae* (rivers draining to E shores of Black Sea), and *E. hellenicus* (Greece).

Distribution The River Danube system, especially the feeder streams.

Habitat Clean streams.

Feeding They attach to host fish with their sucker disc, and ingest dissolved blood and flesh.

Size Usually in the range 20-35cm.

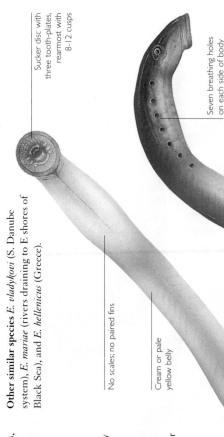

Sucker disc with three tooth-plates, rearmost with 8-12 cusps

Seven breathing holes on each side of body

No scales; no paired fins

Cream or pale yellow belly

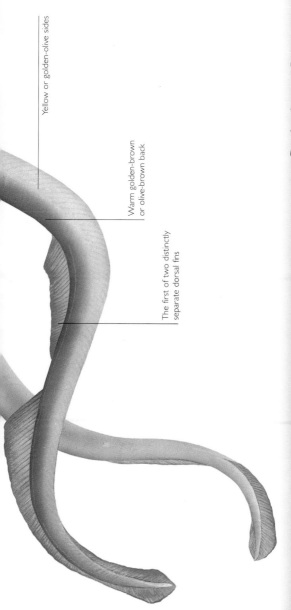

Yellow or golden-olive sides

Warm golden-brown or olive-brown back

The first of two distinctly separate dorsal fins

Sturgeon *Acipenser sturio*

Rarely seen, the sturgeon feeds and grows at sea and spawns in rivers. The rows of bony plates running along an otherwise scaleless body, and their huge size, make sturgeons unmistakable. Caviar is the eggs of sturgeon.

Distribution Recorded from around most of Europe's coast but found spawning regularly in only three rivers (Danube, Gironde, Rioni).

Habitat Lower reaches of clean rivers.

Feeding Bottom feeders (at sea to 60m), taking shrimps, snails and bivalves, worms and fish fry.

Size Up to 3.5m in length, 200+kg in weight.

Other similar species Adriatic sturgeon (*A. naccarii*), Russian sturgeon (*A. guldenstaedti*), ship sturgeon (*A. nudiventris*), stellate sturgeon (*A. stellatus*) and beluga (*Huso huso*) occur in Black, Caspian and Adriatic river systems. Some are farmed for caviar.

Asymmetric tail with longer upper lobe

No scales

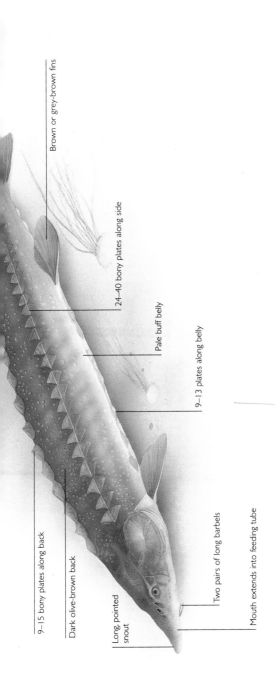

9–15 bony plates along back

Dark olive-brown back

Long, pointed snout

Two pairs of long barbels

Mouth extends into feeding tube

9–13 plates along belly

Pale buff belly

24–40 bony plates along side

Brown or grey-brown fins

Sterlet *Acipenser rutheneus*

The sterlet is the commonest sturgeon, spending all its life in freshwater. It is a popular anglers' quarry. Its relatively small size, fringed barbels, snout and abundant bony plates on an otherwise scaleless skin separate the sterlet from both sturgeon and from the other fish inhabiting the same rivers.

Distribution Eastern Europe, especially rivers draining to the Black and Caspian Seas; introduced to many Russian rivers.

Habitat Clean large and medium-sized rivers.

Feeding Bottom feeder, sucking up a wide range of riverbed invertebrates (mayfly nymphs, caddis and midge larvae, worms, shrimps etc.).

Size Maximum length usually about 80cm, weight about 2.5kg; exceptionally to 1.2m, 15kg.

Asymmetric tail with larger upper lobe

Fins are brown or olive-brown

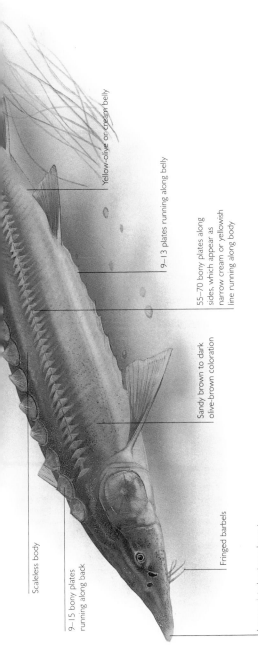

Scaleless body

9–15 bony plates running along back

Long, pointed, upturned snout

Fringed barbels

Sandy brown to dark olive-brown coloration

55–70 bony plates along sides, which appear as narrow cream or yellowish line running along body

9–13 plates running along belly

Yellow-olive or cream belly

Twaite Shad *Alosa fallax*

Shads are members of the herring family and enter freshwater only to spawn (when they can be caught by angling). Thin fatty membranes covering front and rear parts of the eye and the way the lower jaw fits into a notch in the upper are common features of all shads.

Distribution Seas and rivers draining to the seas of western Europe, from S Sweden and Denmark west (including the British Isles) and south to the Mediterranean. There are some isolated lake populations.

Habitat Lower and middle reaches of rivers with clean estuaries.

Feeding Twaite shad is a plankton feeder, taking mainly tiny crustaceans and also larval molluscs and worms. Lake populations eat also planktonic insect larvae.

Size Average length about 30cm, maximum about 50cm; maximum weight 2kg.

Other similar species The marine Black Sea sprat (*Clupeonella cultriventris*) is sometimes found in the lower reaches of Black Sea rivers.

Scale count: 58–70 along body (no lateral line)

Dark blue back shading to gold tinge on sides

Up to 10 dusky spots along body that may be hard to make out

Notched upper jaw into which lower jaw fits

Fine furrows radiating across gill cover

Dorsal fin with 18–21 rays

Anal fin with 19–23 rays

Deeply forked tail with large scales at base

Large head

Flattened sides

The first gill arch has 40–60 short gill rakers

Fatty membrane over front and rear of eye

Silver belly with scales that overlap at a sharp angle

Allis Shad *Alosa alosa*

Allis shad is very similar to twaite Shad (p 36-7), and the presence of only one black spot behind the gill cover is usually considered adequate for identification. However some twaite shad show only one spot and some allis shad two spots. So always check anal fin and (dead fish) gill rakers.

Distribution Seas around western Europe and rivers draining to the sea from Norway and Denmark west (including the British Isles) and south to the Mediterranean.

Habitat Undammed clean rivers that have unpolluted estuaries.

Feeding Allis shad is a filter feeder, taking water in through its mouth and passing it out via the gills whilst filtering out all planktonic animals with its long gill rakers.

Size Average length about 40cm, with a maximum of about 60cm, 2.7kg.

Large eyes with fatty membranes at front and rear

Single, sometimes two, dark spots behind gill cover

Body covered with large scales. Scale count: 70–86 along body (no lateral line)

Dorsal fin with 18–20 rays

Large head with long, equal jaws

Lower jaw fits into notched upper jaw

The first gill arch has 78–130 long gill rakers

Furrows radiating over gill cover

Silvery flattened sides with gold hue

Sharply keeled silver belly

Anal fin with 25–26 rays

Dark blue back

Deeply forked tail fin

Black Sea Shad *Alosa (Caspialosa) pontica*

A typical shad, with fatty membranes covering front and rear of eye, notched upper jaw, and keeled belly with toothed overlapping scales. Most (not all) have a dusky black mark to the rear of the gill cover. This species is found only in the Black Sea.

Distribution Black Sea and rivers draining into it.

Habitat Lower reaches of clean, undammed rivers with unpolluted estuaries.

Feeding Black Sea shad feed on small pelagic animals (mainly crustaceans and tiny fish).

Size Maximum length usually about 30cm, maximum 45cm.

Other similar species Caspian Sea Shad (*A. caspia*) is found only in the Caspian, Volvi shad (*A. macedonica*) from Lake Volvi, Greece, and lesser Black Sea shad (*A. maeotica*) from the Black Sea.

Deeply forked tail fin

Dorsal fin with 16–20 rays

Blue-grey back

Single, round, dusky mark on rear of gill cover

Large head with long, level jaws

Large eyes with fatty membranes at front and rear

Lower jaw fits into notched tip of upper jaw

Furrows radiating across gill cover

The first gill arch has 45–70 fairly long, slender gill rakers.

Scale count: 65–80 along body (no lateral line)

Flattened sides and sharply keeled belly

Long-based anal fin with 18–24 rays

Eel *Anguilla anguilla*

Eels are born in the Sargasso Sea and reach Europe as tiny elvers. Here they grow and then, in autumn, the yellow belly becomes silver, the brown back blackens, and the adult eels head back across the Atlantic to spawn. A commercially important fish and popular anglers' quarry.

Distribution Throughout Europe except for the extreme east.

Habitat Lakes, rivers, canals that are accessible. Although they can colonise isolated pools by crawling overland, they cannot ascend dams or high waterfalls.

Feeding Mainly nocturnal, taking dead and dying animal matter as well as preying on invertebrates and lesser fish.

Size Maximum length usually in the range 30-55cm.

Shown here Yellow eel.

Long dark olive-brown dorsal and anal fins that merge with tail fin

Olive-brown back becomes black when eel prepares to go to sea

Yellow sides and belly become silver when the adult eel prepares to head back to sea

Deeply buried scales

Rounded pectoral fins

Small gill covers just before pectoral fins

Small eyes

Protruding lower jaw

Elvers (transparent, but become pigmented on arrival in Europe)

Pike *Esox lucius*

The pike is one of the largest predatory fish of European freshwaters. Its large powerful jaws enable it to seize relatively large prey, its camouflaged coloration helps it to lie in wait, undetected by its prey, and the positioning of the rear fins allows for fast acceleration. A popular anglers' quarry; an important culinary fish in some parts of Europe.

Distribution Naturally found from the Pyrenees eastwards through most of Europe; introduced Ireland, NW Britain and Iberia.

Habitat Clean rivers, lakes and canals.

Feeding Lesser fish; also aquatic birds, mammals and amphibians. Pike often hunt alone but rest in shoals.

Size Usually 50-80cm long, maximum 1.5m. Weight exceptionally to 25kg.

Dorsal, anal and tail fins are close together and produce fast acceleration

Dorsal fin with 13–18 rays

Olive- or green-brown back

Anal fin with 12–16 rays

Yellow belly

Sides copiously flecked and spotted with yellow

Scale count: 105–130

Long fangs on lower jaw

Small teeth on upper jaw

Long snout with large, powerful jaws

European Mudminnow *Umbra krameri*

This tiny, stockily built fish is rarely seen because it lives in oxygen-starved swamps, ponds and river backwaters where it is usually the only fish present, and is not caught by anglers. It is a shoal fish, drably coloured to camouflage it in its murky environment.

Distribution The River Danube catchment.

Habitat Very weedy and often oxygen-depleted swamps, ponds, sluggish streams and overgrown river backwaters and oxbow lakes.

Feeding Mainly bottom foods, including bloodworms, water hog-lice, aquatic worms,

snails, pea-mussels, small dragonfly nymphs and water-boatmen.

Size Males reach average lengths of 6.5cm, females 8.5cm.

Other similar species The American mudminnow (*U. pygmaea*) has been introduced to weedy pools in France, Holland and N Germany.

Dorsal fin positioned well back with 13–15 rays

Brown and buff sides

Olive-brown back

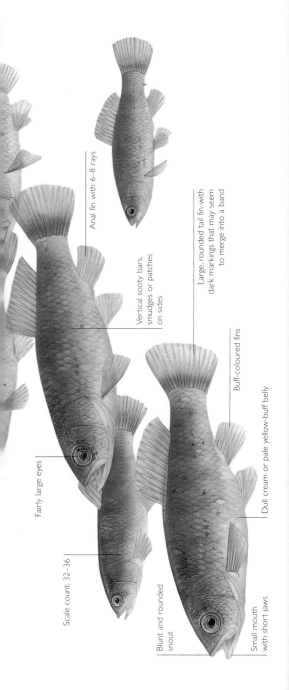

Anal fin with 6–8 rays

Vertical sooty bars, smudges or patches on sides

Large, rounded tail fin with dark markings that may seem to merge into a band

Buff-coloured fins

Dull cream or pale yellow-buff belly

Fairly large eyes

Scale count: 32–36

Blunt and rounded snout

Small mouth with short jaws

Atlantic Salmon *Salmo salar*

The 'King of Fish', the salmon has a high reputation as an anglers' quarry, as a gourmets' delight, and for its remarkable life history. For 1-3 years it lives in the sea as a parr, then goes to sea as a silver smolt. After 1-3 years at sea it returns as a bright silver salmon, but then it gains a spawning coloration (see illustration).

Distribution NW Europe from Spain (formerly Portugal) to arctic Russia, including Iceland and the British Isles.

Habitat Clean rivers; also lakes on river courses.

Feeding Parr feed on river invertebrates; at sea salmon feed on small fish and large invertebrates. On their return to freshwater, salmon do not feed.

Size Adult salmon usually weigh in the range 1.5-10kg, exceptionally over 15kg (in general, the longer at sea the greater the weight).

Shown here Bottom left, parr; front, male; back, female.

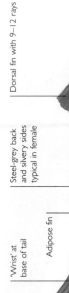

'Wrist' at base of tail

Adipose fin

Forked tail fin

Steel-grey back and silvery sides typical in female

Dorsal fin with 9-12 rays

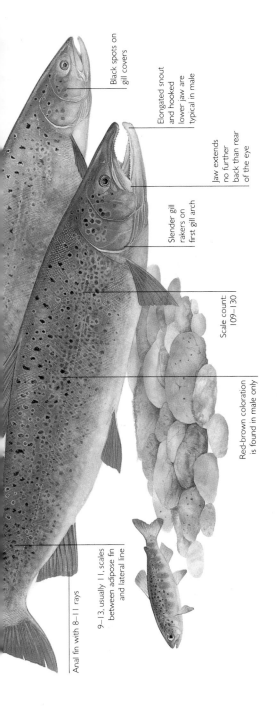

Black spots on gill covers

Elongated snout and hooked lower jaw are typical in male

Jaw extends no further back than rear of the eye

Slender gill rakers on first gill arch

Scale count: 109–130

Red-brown coloration is found in male only

Anal fin with 8–11 rays

9–13, usually 11, scales between adipose fin and lateral line

Brown Trout *Salmo trutta*

The adipose fin marks this species as a salmonid, and the jaw extending beyond the rear of the eye separates it from the salmon, but the brown trout is a highly variable fish. Some migrate to sea as 'sea trout' and return with silver coloration. Others remain in freshwater, and may be brown-and-yellow with red and black spots or drab grey with only a few black spots.

Distribution Throughout most of Europe; where brown trout do not naturally occur they have been introduced both for angling and for food.

Habitat Clean cool rivers and lakes.

Feeding Brown trout eat a range of aquatic insects, flies and lesser fish.

Size Most freshwater trout attain a maximum length of 15-30cm; some lake trout weigh 10+kg; sea trout weigh up to 3kg, exceptionally 5+kg.

Shown here Top, freshwater brown trout; bottom, sea trout.

Adipose fin

Dorsal fin with 11-15 rays

Buff or yellow-brown sides with many black and red spots

Brown back

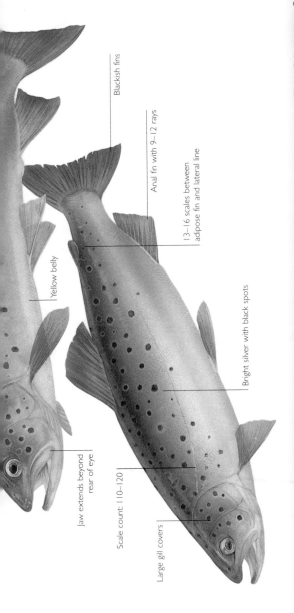

Blackish fins

Anal fin with 9–12 rays

13–16 scales between adipose fin and lateral line

Yellow belly

Bright silver with black spots

Jaw extends beyond rear of eye

Scale count: 110–120

Large gill covers

Marbled Trout *Salmo marmorata*

Although considered by some to be a form of brown trout, this spectacular fish-eating trout is best considered a species in its own right. Almost on the verge of extinction, marbled trout were saved in only one river through the efforts of Slovenian fly-fishers and the State Fishery Department.

Distribution Formerly several rivers draining into the Adriatic Sea; now only the Soca River.

Habitat Clean mountain rivers.

Feeding Juveniles feed on invertebrates, but larger fish feed almost exclusively on grayling.

Size Most attain weights of 3-5kg, but in the past they attained much greater weights: to 10-20kg.

Flattened snout with nostrils pointing upwards

Intricate dark grey or grey-brown and whitish marbling on upper body

Dorsal fin with 11–13 rays

Scale count: 110–120

Large mouth with jaw extending beyond rear of eye

Large gill covers

White belly

Dark grey-black fins

Anal fin with 10–12 rays

13–16 small scales between adipose fin and lateral line

Overall coloration is a medium-grey cast

Huchen *Hucho hucho*

The adipose fin and streamlined build help identify the huchen as a member of the salmon family. The huchen is a very special salmonid, however, having a local distribution and specialised diet, and growing to huge size. Its survival is largely a consequence of its angling popularity.

Distribution River Danube and its tributaries, where pollution and damming have reduced stocks. Introduced into other E European rivers, where populations maintained by hatcheries.

Habitat Clean rivers.

Feeding The huchen is a fish-eater, taking species such as minnows when small and chub and grayling when larger. They tend to be solitary, crepuscular feeders.

Size Today most attain a maximum length of 75cm, weight of 3kg. In the past there were reports of fish to 1.8m and 70kg.

15–17 scales between the adipose fin and lateral line

Grey-black or brown-black tail fin

Silver sides often with copper or pinkish hue

Grey-black or brown-black dorsal fin with 13 rays

Body covered with lots of small, black, X-shaped or rounded spots

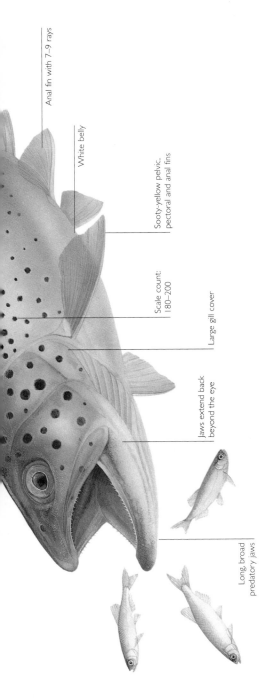

Anal fin with 7–9 rays

White belly

Sooty-yellow pelvic, pectoral and anal fins

Scale count: 180–200

Large gill cover

Jaws extend back beyond the eye

Long, broad predatory jaws

Rainbow Trout *Oncorhynchus mykiss*

The introduced (from N America) rainbow trout is positively separated from the native salmon and trout by its spotted (not uniformly dark) tail fin. Most also have bright pink hues on sides. Some rainbow trout migrate to sea: they are called steelheads. This is a popular anglers' quarry and an important farmed culinary fish.

Distribution Introduced from 1881, the rainbow trout is found throughout most of Europe.

Habitat It breeds in some limestone or chalk rivers; introduced from farms to other rivers and lakes.

Feeding Mainly invertebrates, including tiny planktonic crustaceans that are filtered from the water. In summer seeks fry and other lesser fish.

Size Most feral rainbow trout grow to maximum lengths of 20–35cm, weights of up to 2kg. In farms to 20+kg.

Shown here Top, sea-run steelhead; bottom, resident freshwater rainbow.

Tail fin spotted black on a pale background

Black-spotted silver sides gain rose-pink hue after return to freshwater

Dorsal fin with 10–13 rays

15–16 scales between adipose fin and lateral line

Anal fin with 12–18 rays

Tiny scales.
Scale count: 135–150

Pink bands along sides of black-speckled silvery body and pink patches on gill covers

Large gill covers

Humpback Salmon *Oncorhynchus gorbuscha*

A Pacific salmon, introduced to Europe, that has occasionally been caught in Iceland, Britain and Norway by salmon anglers. On its return from the sea, the fish has a grey-blue back, silver sides and white belly, but it quickly develops a spawning dress.

Distribution Males (right) and females introduced to rivers draining into the White and Barents Seas.

Habitat Clean rivers.

Feeding Feeds on fish and large crustaceans and molluscs at sea; does not feed on return to freshwater.

Size Adults 45–60cm in length, 1.5–2kg weight.

Other similar species Chum salmon (*O. keta*) have been introduced to the same Russian rivers as the humpback; coho salmon (*O. kisutch*) to N France. Both introductions probably failed.

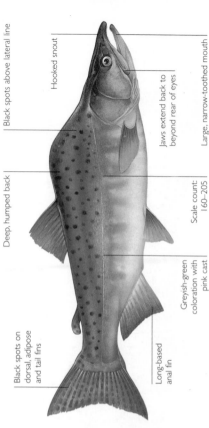

Black spots above lateral line

Hooked snout

Jaws extend back to beyond rear of eyes

Large, narrow-toothed mouth

Scale count: 160–205

Deep, humped back

Black spots on dorsal, adipose and tail fins

Greyish-green coloration with pink cast

Long-based anal fin

Adriatic Salmon *Salmothymus obtusirostris*

This rare little fish is closely related to the Salmo trout and salmon and is thought to be a relict from Ice Age populations. It is most likely to be confused with brown trout and the two can be separated with certainty by the lateral line scale count.

Distribution Rivers and some lakes draining into the eastern side of the Adriatic Sea from Albania northwards.

Habitat Clean rivers.

Feeding Mainly invertebrates, including mayfly and stonefly nymphs, midge and caddis larvae and pupae, and winged flies taken from the water surface.

Size Maximum length in the range 20-25cm; exceptionally longer.

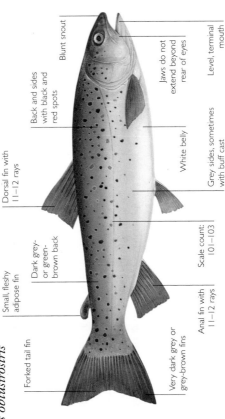

Blunt snout

Back and sides with black and red spots

Jaws do not extend beyond rear of eyes

Level, terminal mouth

White belly

Grey sides, sometimes with buff cast

Dorsal fin with 11-12 rays

Small, fleshy adipose fin

Dark grey- or green-brown back

Scale count: 101-103

Anal fin with 11-12 rays

Forked tail fin

Very dark grey or grey-brown fins

Arctic Charr *Salvelinus alpinus*

Charr are members of the salmon family (with an adipose fin and streamlined build). Most are gaudy fish with diagnostic white-edged bright orange lower fins. Many charr in the arctic are sea-going, returning to freshwater in a silvery livery that rapidly brightens. A popular anglers' quarry.

Distribution Iceland, northern British Isles, Fenno-Scandia and Russia and some alpine lakes, with sea-going populations in Iceland, northern Norway and arctic Russia.

Habitat Cold, clean lakes; also rivers in the far north.

Feeding Mainly invertebrates, though they do take fry and other tiny fish. In lakes, shoals of charr feed by filtering animal plankton from the water.

Size Lake charr grow to about 35cm in length and 0.75kg in weight; sea-run charr are usually in the range 40-55cm, weighing around 1.5kg.

Shown here Top, female; bottom, male in spawning colours.

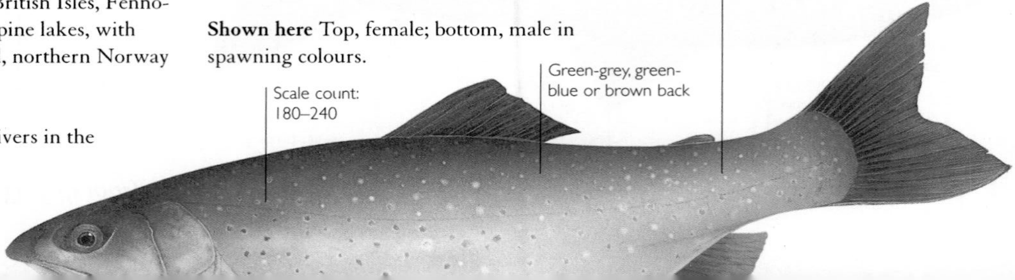

19–22 scales between adipose fin and lateral line

Green-grey, green-blue or brown back

Scale count: 180–240

Tail fin sometimes has a deep red terminal band

Anal fin with 8–13 rays

Pectoral, pelvic and anal fins red or orange with clean-cut, white leading edges

Sides liberally spotted with pale yellow, sometimes bright orange

Dark dorsal fin with 10–15 rays

Lemon-cream, yellow, pale pink-orange or deep orange-red belly

Large gill covers

19–32 gill rakers in first gill arch

Speckled Charr *Salvelinus fontinalis*

Introduced to Europe from North America (where it is called the 'brook trout') in 1884, the speckled charr can be immediately separated from the native arctic charr by the black line separating white and orange on the lower fins and the complex vermiculations on the back.

Distribution A very few feral stocks are established in W France and the Alps. Otherwise the presence of this species depends on releases from fish-farms in Britain, Fenno-Scandia and SE Europe.

Habitat Clean rivers; also introduced to lakes.

Feeding Invertebrates (especially river and lake bed species); larger speckled charr also devour smaller fish.

Size Wild bred average about 25cm in length, maximum 40cm.

Other similar species The mackinaw or lake charr (*S. namaycush*) has been introduced to lakes in southern Scandinavia and the Alps.

Shown here Top, farmed speckled charr; bottom, wild speckled charr.

Slightly forked tail fin

Dorsal fin with 10–14 rays

Anal fin with 9–14 rays

18–25 scales between adipose fin and lateral line

Pectoral, pelvic and anal fins have white leading edges, a clean black line, then red or red-brown

Cream to deep orange-red belly fading to white between lower fins

Scale count: 160–240

The first gill arch has 14–22 gill rakers

Large mouth; jaws extend back slightly behind eyes

Dark olive or olive-green back, dorsal and adipose fins with yellow spots and wavy lines, and red spots with grey-blue borders

Powan (or Schelly or Houting) *Coregonus lavaretus*

The powan is one of three whitefish found in Europe. Silvery-white herring-like fish, their adipose fins link them to the salmon and trout family. In the powan the upper jaw extends beyond the lower; this may be difficult to discern in some isolated populations but is quite distinct in the migratory houting.

Distribution Isolated deep mountain lakes in the Alps and NW Britain; more widespread in NE Europe. The sea-going houting occurs in rivers draining to the Baltic and (very rare) North Sea.

Habitat Clean cold lakes and rivers.

Feeding Lake populations are mainly plankton filter-feeders though, like river powan, they will also take small invertebrates from the bottom and flies from the surface.

Size Most attain lengths of up to 25cm; in arctic lakes reported to 70cm and up to 8kg.

Dorsal fin with 9–15 rays

Blue-grey back

25–44 slender gill rakers on the first gill arch

Small head

White iris

Upper jaw extends beyond lower jaw

Small mouth with no teeth

Silver sides and belly

Scale count: 80–100

Pectoral, pelvic and anal fins are grey with dark tips

Deeply forked tail

Adipose fin

Anal fin with 11–15 rays

Vendace *Coregonus albula*

This typically small silvery whitefish can be separated from the powan by its lower jaw that protrudes beyond the upper, although this can be difficult to discern in some isolated populations. It is an endangered species in Britain, with special legal protection. Elsewhere it occurs in often vast shoals.

Distribution SW Scotland and NW England, and countries bordering the Baltic Sea.

Habitat Mainly cold unproductive lakes, though in some areas also found in rivers connecting lakes.

Feeding Mainly animal plankton which the vendace filter from the water. They will also feed on midge and other pupae rising through the water to hatch, and when plankton is scarce, bottom foods.

Size In some lakes the average length is 10cm, in others 20cm. Exceptionally to 35cm.

Adipose fin

Deep blue-green or blue-grey back

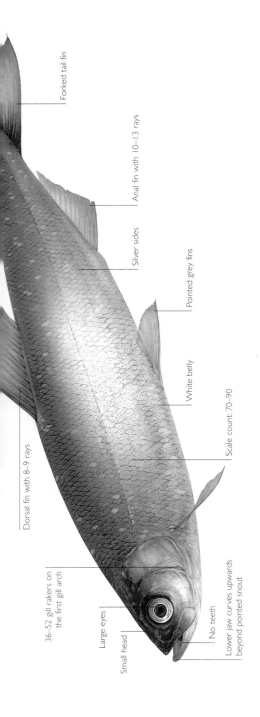

Forked tail fin

Anal fin with 10–13 rays

Silver sides

Pointed grey fins

White belly

Scale count: 70–90

Dorsal fin with 8–9 rays

36–52 gill rakers on the first gill arch

Large eyes

Small head

No teeth

Lower jaw curves upwards beyond pointed snout

Pollan *Coregonus autumnalis*

The pollan is identified from powan and vendace by its upper and lower jaws being level. This is the same whitefish species as the arctic cisco, that occurs in arctic Canada, Alaska and Asiatic Siberia; in Europe it occurs in only four isolated Irish lakes. Commercially fished in Lough Neagh.

Distribution The Irish loughs Neagh, Erne, Ree and Derg (now possibly extinct in the last two).

Habitat Lowland lakes with large populations of midge and planktonic crustaceans.

Feeding Planktonic crustaceans (e.g. *Daphnia* and *Bythotrephes*) and midge pupae rising to hatch are filtered from the water. Adult midges may be

taken from the water surface and small invertebrates from the lake bed.

Size Average length in range 20-30cm.

Other similar species Inconnu (*Stenodus leucichthys*) occurs in arctic rivers draining to the White Sea eastwards.

Deeply forked tail

Round, fleshy adipose fin

Dorsal fin with 10-12 rays

Medium to dark grey dorsal, adipose and tail fins

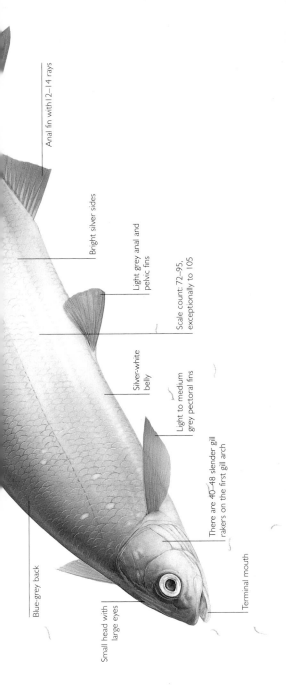

Anal fin with 12–14 rays

Bright silver sides

Light grey anal and pelvic fins

Scale count: 72–95, exceptionally to 105

Silver-white belly

Light to medium grey pectoral fins

There are 40–48 slender gill rakers on the first gill arch

Terminal mouth

Blue-grey back

Small head with large eyes

Grayling *Thymallus thymallus*

With its streamlined build and huge brightly coloured dorsal fin, the grayling is rightly the 'Lady of the stream'. Unlike most river salmonids, it is a shoal fish and, whereas salmon, trout, charr and whitefish spawn in the period late autumn to late winter, grayling spawn in late spring. Over much of Europe it is the most popular fly-fishers' quarry.

Distribution SE England (introduced to W and N England and S Scotland) and SE France eastwards through much of Fenno-Scandia and C Europe into Russia.

Habitat Mainly clean rivers but also lakes, especially in the north of its range.

Feeding Mainly river and lake bed invertebrates, but grayling will readily rise to take flies from the water surface.

Size Most attain lengths of 25-30cm; exceptionally over 45cm.

Huge dorsal fin, with 17–28 rays, speckled or banded with black, green and orange- or purple-red

Underslung mouth

Large eye with
pear-shaped pupil

Large scales run in horizontal
lines down the body.
Scale count: 75–90

Pale cream belly sometimes
edged with buff

Anal fin with
9–12 rays

Adipose fin; 9–12 scales
between adipose fin and
lateral line

Smelt *Osmerus eperlanus*

A distant relation to the salmonids, the smelt is a marine fish that enters the lower reaches of rivers in spring to spawn. A small silvery-white fish, it is often abundant in estuaries and is then a major food for fish-eating birds and other fish including sea trout and sea bass.

Feeding Small smelts feed on plankton; larger smelts feed on shrimps, small crabs and prawns, and on the fry of other fish.

Size Maximum length in the range 18–20cm.

Distribution Coastal waters around southern Britain, and from the Bay of Biscay eastwards to and around the Baltic to southern Norway. There are a few 'land-locked' lake populations.

Habitat Clean estuaries and lower freshwater river reaches; also clean cool lakes.

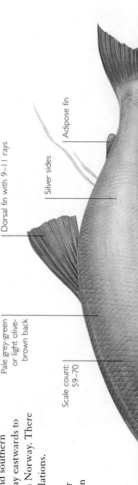

Scale count: 59–70

Pale grey-green or light olive-brown back

Dorsal fin with 9–11 rays

Silver sides

Adipose fin

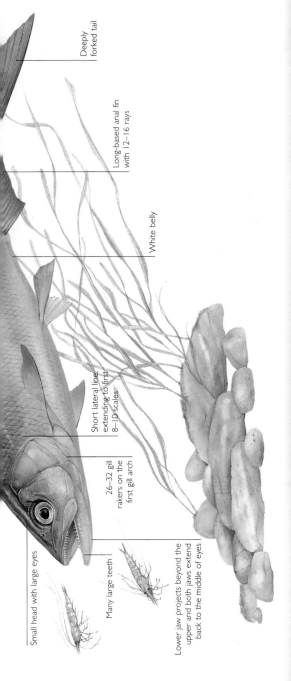

Deeply forked tail

Long-based anal fin with 12–16 rays

White belly

Short lateral line, extending to first 8–10 scales

26–32 gill rakers on the first gill arch

Small head with large eyes

Many large teeth

Lower jaw projects beyond the upper and both jaws extend back to the middle of eyes

Carp *Cyprinus carpio*

This large cyprinid has been bred in fish farms to produce the fully scaled king carp, the almost scaleless leather carp, and the mirror carp with large scales along the sides and on the back. The wild carp is similar to the farmed king carp, but slower growing and more slender in build. Popular amongst anglers; a common table fish.

Distribution Native to SE Europe, carp have been introduced to all Europe except for Iceland, N Scotland and N Fenno-Scandia.

Habitat Lowland lakes, canals and slow weedy rivers.

Feeding Mainly a bottom feeder on invertebrates and weed, although carp will rise to take seeds and fruits fallen from overhanging vegetation.

Size Most attain a length in range 60-70cm, weight 4-6kg; exceptionally over 20kg.

Shown here Leather carp (right), Common carp (below), Mirror carp (bottom left).

Almost scaleless body

Dark brown or grey dorsal fin with 18–22 rays (the first is a strong, toothed spine)

Broad, powerful
tail fin

Anal fin with 4–6 rays

Pectoral, pelvic and anal
fins and lower lobe of tail
fin often have red tinge

Bronze-brown overall coloration
with dark olive-brown back

Scale count: 35–39 in
wild carp and king carp

Two tiny barbels
on upper lip

Two longer barbels at
each corner of mouth

Large scales only on
back and along sides

Light olive, yellow
or cream belly

Crucian Carp *Carassius carassius*

This small carp can be instantly identified from immature common carp by its lack of barbels. Small weedy ponds, where low oxygen levels would kill most cyprinids, often have huge populations of stunted crucian carp. Commonly caught by anglers, but of no culinary value.

Distribution A native of C and E Europe (but not the far N), crucian carp have been introduced to Britain, France and Spain.

Habitat Canals and weedy lowland lakes and ponds; occasionally slow rivers.

Feeding Almost exclusively a bottom feeder on aquatic worms, midge larvae, water hog-lice and snails, though in summer they will take plankton from mid-water.

Size In small ponds maximum length 8-10cm; larger waters usually 25-30cm.

Dark grey-brown, long-based convex dorsal fin with 14–21 rays, the first of which is serrated

Golden-brown overall coloration with dark olive- or ruddy-brown back

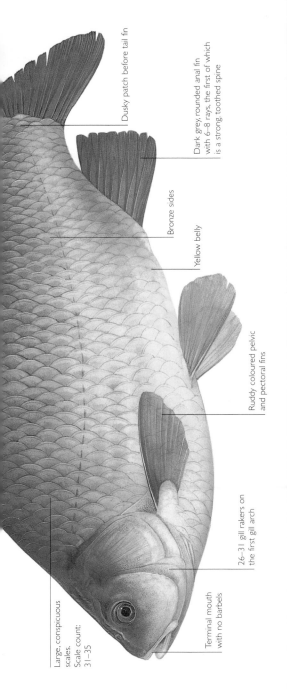

Dusky patch before tail fin

Dark grey; rounded anal fin with 6–8 rays, the first of which is a strong, toothed spine

Bronze sides

Yellow belly

Ruddy coloured pelvic and pectoral fins

26–31 gill rakers on the first gill arch

Terminal mouth with no barbels

Large, conspicuous scales. Scale count: 31–35

Gibel Carp/Goldfish *Carassius auratus*

The goldfish and its many fancy forms were bred from the wild gibel carp, a species that closely resembles the crucian carp. In the crucian the dorsal fin is convex, in the gibel concave or straight; check also scale counts and pharyngeal teeth. Goldfish will sometimes revert back to the drab gibel coloration.

Distribution Gibel carp occur through E Europe (not in N) and have been introduced to Germany and Holland. Goldfish are sometimes released as unwanted 'pets'.

Habitat Weedy ponds and canals.

Feeding Animal plankton, midge larvae, water hog-lice, snails and other bottom invertebrates, occasionally flies from the surface; also weed.

Size In wild gibels usually 10–20cm, exceptionally over 30cm in length.

Shown here Wild gibel carp (top), Goldfish.

Dark grey-brown, long-based dorsal fin with 16–21 rays, the first of which is hard and toothed

Dull green-brown back

Silvery sides with yellow tinge

Anal fin with 5–6 rays, the first of which is a toothed spine

Dull white or cream belly

Light grey pectoral, pelvic, anal and tail fins

Large, rounded tail with a slight fork

Small head with level mouth

Slightly upturned jaws with no barbels

Large, conspicuous scales. Scale count: 28–31

35–38 gill rakers on first gill arch

Chub *Leuciscus cephalus*

Because it is so widespread through Europe, occurs often in big shoals, grows to a fairly large size and will eat just about anything, the chub is one of the most popular anglers' fish. Small chub may be confused with large dace (p 84-5); check dorsal and anal fins.

Distribution Throughout Europe other than N Fenno-Scandia, Iceland, Ireland, N Scotland, S Spain and S Italy.

Habitat Mainly the middle and lower reaches of rivers, though occasionally found in lakes.

Feeding Chub will eat anything they can swallow, including weed, fruit, seeds, bottom invertebrates, flies on the surface, and land creatures (e.g. slugs) that have fallen in the river. Also amphibians and lesser fish.

Size Average maximum length 40cm, weight 2kg; exceptionally to over 7kg.

Other similar species Black Sea Chub (*L. borysthenicus*) occurs only in lower reaches of rivers draining into Black Sea.

Blunt snout

Large mouth

Scale count: 44–46

Dusky silver sides, often with a brown or bronze sheen

Pelvic, anal and sometimes pectoral fins are yellowish; may appear red in water

Silvery white or cream belly

Anal fin with 8–10 rays (the first is sometimes a strong toothed spine) and a convex free edge

Dark grey tail

Dorsal fin with 8–10 rays and a convex free edge

Dark grey-brown or olive-brown back

Large scales with conspicuous dusky grey margins

Ide (or Orfe) *Leuciscus idus*

The ide is a common E European fish that has never penetrated NW or S Europe. It could be confused with a small chub (p 80-1). The golden orfe is a cultivated form of the ide and is commonly found in ornamental ponds; save for its colour, its structure is as the wild ide.

Distribution Europe west to Germany and Holland, but not the far N or S. Wild ide have been introduced to lakes in S and C England.

Habitat Lowland lakes, and the lower reaches of rivers including brackish estuaries.

Feeding River and lake invertebrates including caddis and midge larvae, stonefly and mayfly nymphs, freshwater shrimps and snails; also crabs, shrimps and marine worms from estuaries. Large ide eat lesser fish.

Size Average length about 25cm, weight 500g; maximum 40cm, 1.25kg, exceptionally larger.

Shown here Golden orfe variety (top), Wild ide (bottom).

Distinct lateral line (straight or slightly concave)

Blunt snout

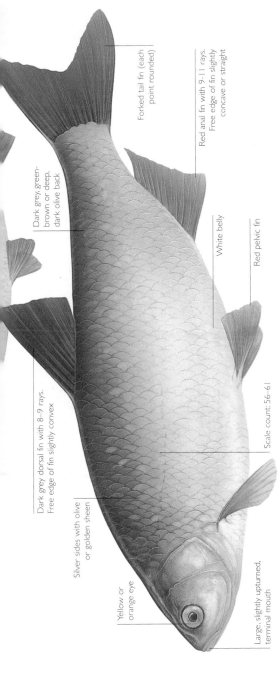

Forked tail fin (each point rounded)

Red anal fin with 9–11 rays. Free edge of fin slightly concave or straight

Dark grey, green-brown or deep, dark olive back

White belly

Red pelvic fin

Dark grey dorsal fin with 8–9 rays. Free edge of fin slightly convex

Scale count: 56–61

Silver sides with olive or golden sheen

Yellow or orange eye

Large, slightly upturned, terminal mouth

Dace *Leuciscus leuciscus*

The dace is a small, silvery fish that sometimes occurs in huge shoals in the lower reaches of rivers. It is sometimes confused for a small chub (p 80–1); cheek eye and dorsal and anal fins. It is a major food of piscivorous river birds and fish, and is a fairly popular anglers' fish.

Distribution England and France eastwards through Europe except for the extreme S and N. Introduced to S Ireland.

Habitat Mainly the lower and middle reaches of rivers, though found occasionally in lakes and canals where introduced by anglers.

Feeding Mainly river bed invertebrates (eg blackfly and midge larvae); also flies from the surface (hatched midges, mayflies, caddisflies). Will also graze algae from rocks.

Size Average maximum length in range 15–25cm, weight to 250g; exceptionally to 30cm.

Silvery sides

Dark grey dorsal fin with 7–8 rays. Outer edge of fin is concave

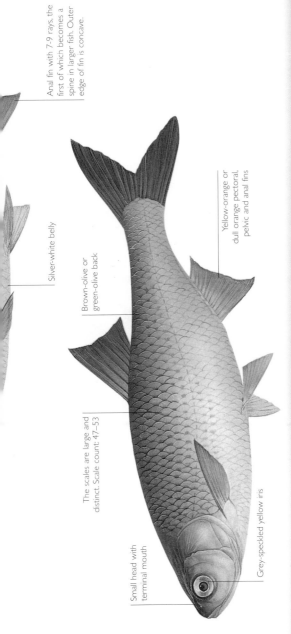

Anal fin with 7-9 rays, the first of which becomes a spine in larger fish. Outer edge of fin is concave.

Silver-white belly

Brown-olive or green-olive back

Yellow-orange or dull orange pectoral, pelvic and anal fins

The scales are large and distinct. Scale count: 47–53

Small head with terminal mouth

Grey-speckled yellow iris

Balkan Dace *Leuciscus svallise*

This small silvery dace replaces the common dace (p 84-5) in rivers draining into the Adriatic. Lateral line scale count varies from one river system to the next, and some scientists regard these as separate species. Balkan dace often occur in large shoals and provide food to many predators.

Distribution Rivers draining to the Adriatic from Slovenia south to the Vijose River in S Albania.

Habitat Clean limestone rivers.

Feeding Invertebrates, including bottom species (eg nymphs and larvae) and winged flies from the surface.

Size Usual length 15-20cm; exceptionally to 25cm.

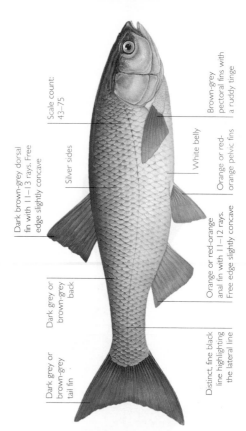

Dark brown-grey dorsal fin with 11–13 rays. Free edge slightly concave

Scale count: 43–75

Silver sides

White belly

Brown-grey pectoral fins with a ruddy tinge

Orange or red-orange pelvic fins

Dark grey or brown-grey back

Dark grey or brown-grey tail fin

Orange or red-orange anal fin with 11–12 rays. Free edge slightly concave

Distinct, fine black line highlighting the lateral line

Soufie *Leuciscus souffia*

The soufie is a small dace-like fish living in mountain streams in C and S Europe. It is a little-known fish that has declined over parts of its range because of damming of the rivers.

Distribution Alpine regions of S Germany, N Italy, Switzerland and Austria, S from the Julian Alps to Bosnia and in the Transylvanian Alps of Romania.

Habitat Clean rivers and streams to 2200m.

Feeding River bed invertebrates, including insect larvae and nymphs. Also some surface flies.

Size Average length 10-12cm, exceptionally to 15cm.

Other similar species A soufie from W Greece has been named *L. pleurobipunctatus*.

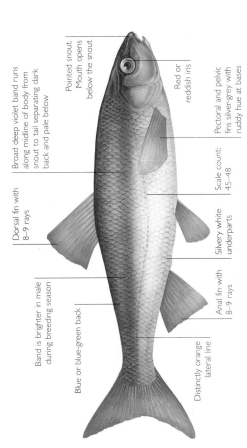

Pointed snout. Mouth opens below the snout

Broad deep violet band runs along midline of body from snout to tail separating dark back and pale below

Dorsal fin with 8–9 rays

Red or reddish iris

Scale count: 45–48

Pectoral and pelvic fins silver-grey with ruddy hue at bases

Silvery white underparts

Band is brighter in male during breeding season

Blue or blue-green back

Anal fin with 8–9 rays

Distinctly orange lateral line

Zeige *Pelecus cultratus*

With its straight back and curved belly, long anal fin and tiny dorsal fin, and markedly upturned mouth, this is one of the most unmistakable of cyprinids. It is also a great migrant, feeding in brackish estuaries and swimming far upstream to spawn.

Distribution Two separate populations. One in countries bordering the S Baltic (Denmark, Poland, Baltic States and S Finland and Sweden) is now endangered. The second is based in rivers draining to the northern coasts of Black and Caspian Seas.

Habitat Clean rivers and estuaries.

Feeding Immatures feed on a variety of river invertebrates; adults feed almost exclusively on small fish.

Size Average length in the range 25-35cm, weight about 1.5kg; exceptionally to over 60cm.

Pale grey tail fin streaked with yellow

Pale grey dorsal fin streaked with yellow with 7–8 rays

Silvery coloration with light blue-green or grey-green back

Short snout

Long-based anal fin with 24–29 rays

Reddish anal and pelvic fins

Silvery sides with pink or red sheen

Scale count: 95–115

Long pale grey pectoral fins streaked with yellow

Large, strongly upturned mouth

Large, prominent eyes

Wavy lateral line meandering from top of gill cover to base of tail fin

Silver-white belly with light pink sheen

Moderlieschen *Leucaspius delineatus*

The moderlieschen is a tiny fish that occurs often in huge shoals. Its German name means 'motherless', and comes from the way shoals may suddenly appear in what was a fishless pool, presumably carried there as eggs on the feet of waterfowl.

Distribution Through Europe from Belgium eastwards, though not Fenno-Scandia, N Russia, Greece and Italy.

Habitat Weedy ponds and small lakes, margins of weedy rivers and man-made canals, drainage channels and ditches.

Feeding Tiny zooplankton (e.g. *Daphnia*), midge pupae and some flies taken at the water surface.

Size Average maximum length in the range 8-10cm; exceptionally to 12cm.

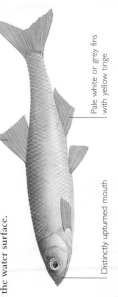

Dorsal fin with 8-9 rays

Pale white or grey fins with yellow tinge

Distinctly upturned mouth

Silvery white belly

Scale count:
44–48 along sides

Large, deeply
forked tail fin

Bright silver sides with
silver-blue iridescent stripe

Anal fin with 11–14 rays

Proportionally large
head with large eyes

Protruding lower jaw

Sharply keeled belly

Olive-green or
blue-green back

Short lateral
line

Roach *Rutilus rutilus*

One of Europe's commonest fish and popular anglers' quarry, roach are sometimes confused with rudd (p 96-7). Check scale counts, iris colour and mouth shape. Also front of dorsal fin base is level with base of pelvic fin in roach, well to rear of pelvic fin base in rudd.

Distribution France and S and E England eastwards into Russia, but not far N and S. Introduced to W Britain and Ireland.

Habitat Small ponds and large lakes, canals and slow rivers.

Feeding Shoal fish, feeding on weed, bottom invertebrates (eg midge larvae, water hog-lice and snails), and in mid-water on insect pupae rising to hatch.

Size Often stunted in ponds (10-15cm in length), but to 25-35cm and 0.5-1.2kg elsewhere; exceptionally to 2kg.

Dull blue-grey, dark olive or olive-brown back

High, grey-brown dorsal fin with 9–13 rays

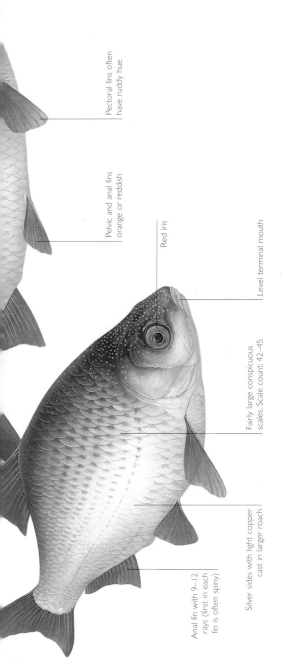

Pectoral fins often have ruddy hue

Pelvic and anal fins orange or reddish

Red iris

Level terminal mouth

Fairly large conspicuous scales. Scale count: 42–45

Anal fin with 9–12 rays (first in each fin is often spiny)

Silver sides with light copper cast in larger roach

Danube Roach *Rutilus pigus*

This is one of three roach species found only in SE Europe, and is most readily identified by its larger lateral line scale count. It is a slender silvery fish, often occurring in large shoals.

Distribution Two separate populations, one in Italy's Po river system, and one in the Danube headwaters from S Switzerland eastwards.

Habitat Slow river pools.

Feeding Water weed and algae; also larvae of blackfly, midge, freshwater shrimp, snails etc.

Size Average length 10–12cm; maximum to 20cm.

Other similar species Pearl roach (*R. frisii*) occurs in the Danube and other rivers draining to the Black Sea. Adriatic roach (*R. rubilio*) occurs in rivers draining to the Adriatic.

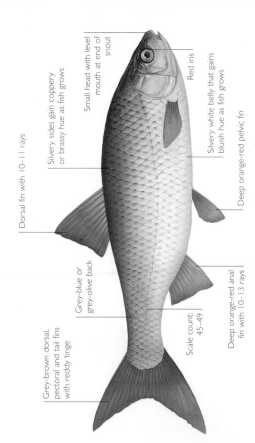

Small head with level mouth at end of snout

Red iris

Silvery sides gain coppery or brassy hue as fish grows

Dorsal fin with 10–11 rays

Grey-blue or grey-olive back

Silvery white belly that gains bluish hue as fish grows

Deep orange-red pelvic fin

Grey-brown dorsal, pectoral and tail fins with reddy tinge

Scale count: 45–49

Deep orange-red anal fin with 10–13 rays

Escalo Roach *Rutilus arcasii*

The escalo is one of three species of roach found only in the Iberian Peninsula. They are very similar to each other; the easiest way to separate them is by distribution and by (overlapping) scale counts.

Distribution Escalo roach occur throughout Portugal and W Spain, but not the far S.

Habitat Big rivers and deeper pools of small streams.

Feeding Insectivorous shoal fish, taking blackfly and midge larvae and pupae, mayfly nymphs, small crustaceans and snails from the river bed.

Size Average maximum length 12–13cm.

Other similar species Calandino roach (*R. alburnoides*) occurs in rivers of SW Spain and S Portugal, pardillo roach (*R. lemmingii*) in S Spain.

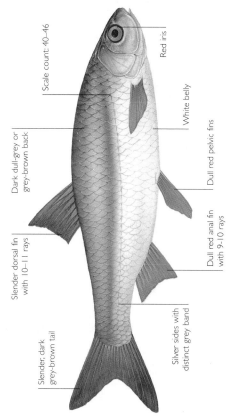

Scale count: 40–46

Red iris

Dark dull-grey or grey-brown back

White belly

Slender dorsal fin with 10–11 rays

Dull red pelvic fins

Slender, dark grey-brown tail

Dull red anal fin with 9–10 rays

Silver sides with distinct grey band

Rudd *Scardinius erythrophthalmus*

Many anglers consider the rudd to be the most beautiful of cyprinids. Though sometimes confused with the roach (see p 92-3) the bright blood-red fins and coppery sides are striking. Its upturned mouth is an adaptation for surface feeding.

Distribution France and SE Britain eastwards through Europe except for the far N; introduced to NW Britain and Ireland.

Habitat Ponds and weedy lowland lakes and canals; also slow rivers.

Feeding Food from below the surface (weed, and small invertebrates), as well as midges and other small flies from the surface.

Size Often stunted (length 8-12cm) in small waters; to 35cm and exceptionally 45cm elsewhere.

Other related species The Greek rudd (*S. graecus*) from Lakes Yliki and Paralimni and the Acheloos rudd (*S. acarnanicus*) from Archeloos River and Lakes Trichonis and Lyssimachia (Greece) may better be considered races of the rudd.

Reddish dorsal fin with 8-10 rays, the first of which is often a sharp spine

Sides silver in tiny rudd, copper in larger ones

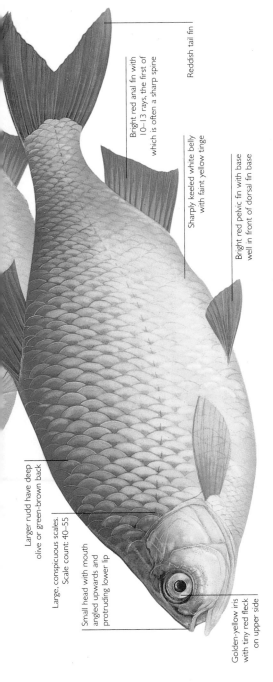

Reddish tail fin

Bright red anal fin with 10–13 rays, the first of which is often a sharp spine

Sharply keeled white belly with faint yellow tinge

Bright red pelvic fin with base well in front of dorsal fin base

Larger rudd have deep olive or green-brown back

Large, conspicuous scales. Scale count: 40–55

Small head with mouth angled upwards and protruding lower lip

Golden-yellow iris with tiny red fleck on upper side

Bitterling *Rhodeus sericeus*

A small fish with a remarkable breeding system. The female lays her eggs through an ovipositor tube into freshwater mussels, which protect the eggs from predators. It is an increasingly common garden pond and aquarium fish.

Distribution From N France eastwards through Russia, but not S and N Europe; introduced to S and C England.

Habitat Small weedy lakes, canals and very slow rivers with freshwater mussels.

Feeding Microscopic algae, silkweed and waterweed; also tiny aquatic invertebrates (eg midge larvae and worms).

Size Usual maximum length 6cm, exceptionally to 8.5cm.

Shown here Female during breeding season (left), male during breeding season.

Long-based bright orange-red dorsal fin with 8–10 rays (first often a sharp spine)

Large tail fin

Pale grey fins with orange tinge

Bright silver or iridescent blue-green line along middle of body

Grey-olive or olive-brown back

Bright orange-red, long-based anal fin with 8–11 rays (first often a sharp spine)

Pure white leading edges to pelvic fins

Bright silver sides with iridescent light purple or pinkish hue

Scale count: 34–38 along sides

Large, prominent eyes – gold iris with red fleck on upper surface

Small head with white tubercles

Slightly upturned, terminal mouth

Silver sides with slight purple hue

Silvery white belly

Ovipositor – tube to deposit eggs in freshwater mussels

Minnow *Phoxinus phoxinus*

Minnows are widespread and often abundant shoal fish in rivers and lakes. Tiny fish, they are amongst the most important foods of several species of piscivorous birds and larger fish. Males in breeding dress might be confused with male three-spined sticklebacks (p 156-7).

Distribution Throughout Europe from France and SE Britain eastwards except for northern Fenno-Scandia, Italy and Greece; introduced to NW Britain and Ireland.

Habitat Clean fast-flowing rivers and lakes.

Feeding Mainly minute invertebrates taken from the river bed, but shoals will also rise to drag down and tear apart winged flies from the water surface.

Size Maximum length in the range 6-9cm.

Shown here Breeding male (top left) and females and/or immatures in shoal.

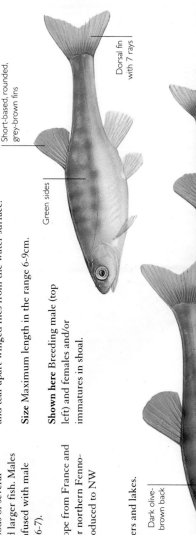

Dorsal fin with 7 rays

Short-based, rounded, grey-brown fins

Green sides

Dark olive-brown back

Anal fin with 6–7 rays

Light olive-brown sides with dark blotches

Lateral line appears broken between dorsal and tail fins

White belly

Scale count: 80–95

Red pelvic and pectoral fins

Black throat

Deep red belly

Blunt-snouted head with slightly upturned mouth

Swamp Minnow *Phoxinus percnurus*

Swamp minnows are slightly stouter and less slender than the minnow. They are also less well known, partly because of their restricted range and habitat, and partly because they are considered by most people to be of no economic significance.

Distribution Poland eastwards into Russia.

Habitat Small weedy pools and shallow lake margins, and overgrown river backwaters.

Feeding Shoal fish that will take any invertebrate they can swallow, from planktonic crustaceans (eg *Daphnia*) to water hog-lice and small snails.

Size Usual maximum length 10–12cm.

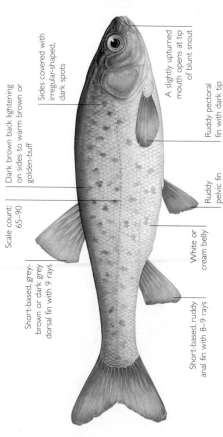

Dark brown back lightening on sides to warm brown or golden-buff

Sides covered with irregular-shaped, dark spots

A slightly upturned mouth opens at tip of blunt snout

Ruddy pectoral fin with dark tip

Scale count: 65–90

Short-based, grey-brown or dark grey dorsal fin with 9 rays

Ruddy pelvic fin

White or cream belly

Short-based, ruddy anal fin with 8–9 rays

Spanish Minnowcarp *Phoxinellus hispanicus*

This tiny, slender fish is one of the least-known and most endangered of European vertebrates with a restricted distribution. The dark back and yellow underparts, separated by a distinct black line, make identification easy.

Distribution River systems Guadalquivir and Guadiana in S Iberia.

Habitat Clean rivers.

Feeding Midge larvae, tiny crustaceans and algae obtained from the river bed.

Size Average length about 5cm.

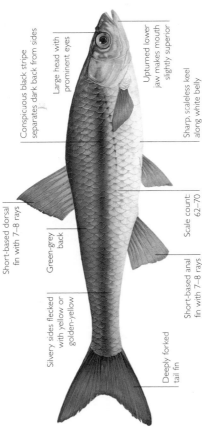

Conspicuous black stripe separates dark back from sides

Large head with prominent eyes

Upturned lower jaw makes mouth slightly superior

Sharp, scaleless keel along white belly

Short-based dorsal fin with 7–8 rays

Green-grey back

Scale count: 62–70

Silvery sides flecked with yellow or golden-yellow

Short-based anal fin with 7–8 rays

Deeply forked tail fin

Bream (Bronze Bream) *Abramis brama*

The bream is a large, flat-sided cyprinid and the slimiest of European fish. Its size, and the way it often occurs in large shoals, makes it a very popular anglers' fish. It is also an important culinary fish. Smaller (sometimes called 'skimmer') bream are more silvery in colour, and may be confused with silver bream (p 110-1).

Distribution France and S and E England eastwards throughout Europe into Russia, but not the far N or S. Introduced to W Britain and Ireland.

Habitat Shallow lowland lakes, slow muddy rivers and canals.

Feeding Bream are bottom feeders, sucking up small animals (midge larvae, worms, snails, pea mussels, water hog-lice etc.) and often disturbing clouds of mud that may be seen at the surface.

Size Maximum length usually in range 50-60cm, weight 2.5-3kg.

Dark brown or grey-brown back

Grey or grey-brown dorsal fin is set well back on body with 9 rays

Light brown or bronze sides

Small eyes with diameter less than or same as length of snout

Small head

Low mouth extends like bellows into a feeding tube

Long-based, grey or grey-brown anal fin with 23–31 branched rays

Yellow, cream or buff belly

Pale grey pectoral and pelvic fins with darker tips

Small scales covered in slime. Scale count: 49–60

Blue Bream (or Zope) *Abramis ballerus*

The blue bream is a much smaller fish than the bream with a more restricted range. It also has quite different feeding system (see below). Because of this feeding system it is not usually sought by anglers, and is rarely eaten. If identification in doubt, check anal fin ray and lateral line scale count and eye size.

Distribution N Germany and S Sweden eastwards through Poland and Baltic States to Russia.

Habitat Reservoirs, lakes and slowest weedy river stretches.

Feeding Feeds by filtering planktonic crustaceans from mid-water. It will also take insect larvae from weeds.

Size Maximum length usually in range 25–30cm, weight about 400g; exceptionally to 45cm, 500g.

Short-based, long and slender grey dorsal fin set high on body with 8–9 rays

Dark blue-green or dark blue-grey back

Very deeply
forked grey tail

Long-based, grey anal
fin with 36–46 rays

Silver-grey sides sometimes
with yellow hue

White belly with orange-buff
tinge around pectoral fins

Grey pectoral or pelvic fins
with buff or yellow bases

Scale count: 66–74

Eye diameter
equal to snout
length

Terminal mouth; lower lip
curves up slightly

Danube Bream *Abramis sapa*

The Danube bream is the smallest of the bream species, and rapid certain identification is made from the others by the much longer lower lobe compared with upper lobe of the tail fin (equal in the others) and the large eye. It is a shoaling bottom-feeding fish.

Distribution Besides the Danube system, this bream is also found in other rivers draining into the Black and Caspian Seas.

Habitat Wide slow river reaches including the upper estuary, with mud and silt beds.

Feeding Midge larvae, aquatic worms, crustaceans, snails and pea mussels are amongst the foods obtained by rooting on the river bed.

Size Average length in range 15-20cm, exceptionally to 30cm and a weight of 750g.

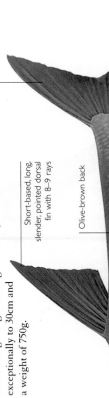

Deeply forked grey-brown tail fin with larger lower lobe

Short-based, long, slender, pointed dorsal fin with 8–9 rays

Olive-brown back

Large eyes with a diameter greater than length of snout

Small head with blunt snout

Terminal mouth

Long-based, grey-brown anal fin with 36–48 rays

White belly

Silver sides, often with yellow or orange tinge

Scale count: 48–52

Silver Bream *Blicca bjoerkna*

Although it is possible to misidentify this as a silvery immature specimen of the other bream species, the lack of slime on the body, large eyes and the grey-tipped reddish lower fins allow rapid and certain identification. It is less of a bottom-feeder than the other bream.

Distribution France and SE England eastwards through Europe into Russia except for the far N and S.

Habitat Weedy lowland ponds and lakes, canals, drains and slow rivers.

Feeding Hog-lice, snails and pea mussels, aquatic worms and midge larvae are taken from the river bed; but silver bream will also take species such as water-boatmen and zooplankton from weedy open water.

Size Maximum length usually 20-25cm, weighing 0.4-0.7kg; exceptionally to 30cm, 1.1kg.

Short-based, dark grey dorsal fin with 8–9 lighter rays

Light olive-brown or grey-brown back

Long-based, dark grey anal fin with 19–24 lighter rays, the first of which may be a spine

Silver or silvery sides

Reddish pectoral and pelvic fins with grey tips

Scale count: 43–55

White belly

Blunt snout and semi-terminal mouth that is slightly upturned and positioned low on snout

Small head and large eyes with a diameter larger than snout length

Zahrte *Vimba vimba*

The illustration is of an unmistakable male in spawning colours. Outside breeding the sides and belly are yellow-buff and the back paler. The underslung mouth and highly sensitive fleshy snout indicate that this cyprinid, that may travel hundreds of kilometres each year within the river, is a bottom-feeder. Commercially fished in E Europe.

Distribution N Germany and S Sweden eastwards to S Finland, Baltic States and Russia, and S to the Black Sea.

Habitat Lower reaches of large rivers down to the estuary, including lakes on the river.

Feeding Tubificid and polychaete worms, a variety of crustaceans and molluscs and insect larvae are grubbed from the bottom as the zahrte shoals move through the river system.

Size Usual maximum length about 30cm, weight 500g; exceptionally to 50cm, 1kg.

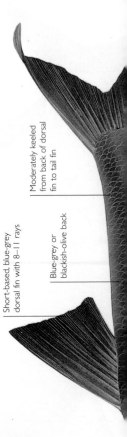

Short-based, blue-grey dorsal fin with 8–11 rays

Blue-grey or blackish-olive back

Moderately keeled from back of dorsal fin to tail fin

Deeply forked blue-grey tail

Moderately long-based, yellow or orange-yellow anal fin with 17–22 rays

Sides flattened

Bright orange-red belly

Small scales. Scale count: 51–64

Yellow or yellow-orange pectoral and pelvic fins

Small head dominated by fleshy, conical, pointed snout

Underslung, horseshoe-shaped mouth with a protruding upper jaw

Bleak *Alburnus alburnus*

The tiny bleak occurs often in shoals so vast that anglers can catch a fish every 10 seconds throughout a five-hour competition! Their silvery scales have been used in the manufacture of nail varnish and synthetic pearls.

Distribution France and SE England eastwards to Russia, but not N Fenno-Scandia and arctic Russia or Italy and countries bordering the Adriatic.

Habitat Clean slow-flowing rivers and some lakes.

Feeding Bleak shoals feed mainly in mid-water on insect pupae and nymphs rising to hatch and on flies on the surface. They will also take planktonic crustaceans and plant material such as algae and weed leaves.

Size Maximum length usually in the range 12-15cm; exceptionally to 18cm.

Other similar species White bleak (*A. albidus*) occur in N Italy and countries bordering the Adriatic S to Greece.

Small head, with very large eye twice the snout length

Bright silver sides and belly

Scale count 46–55; scales very easily detach

Off-white pectoral and pelvic fins, sometimes with a slight reddish hue at base (orange during spawning season)

Upturned mouth with protruding lower jaw

Blue-green back

Short-based, pale grey dorsal fin with 8–9 rays

Distinctly keeled belly

Deeply forked, pale grey tail fin

Long-based, off-white anal fin with 17–21 rays

Danube Bleak *Chalcalburnus chalcoides*

Danube bleak is often found within its range in similar water to the bleak. In this species the scales do not easily detach as in bleak, the eye is smaller, the lateral line scale count is greater and the sides are more flattened. It too is a mid-water shoal fish.

Distribution Rivers draining to the Black and Caspian Seas; also in alpine lakes in Austria.

Habitat Slow-flowing, often weedy rivers, and clean lakes.

Feeding Danube bleak feed mainly on midge pupae and planktonic crustaceans in mid-water and adult midges on the surface.

Size Usual maximum length 15-20cm, occasionally to 25cm and exceptionally larger.

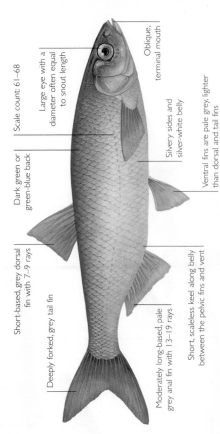

Scale count: 61–68

Large eye with a diameter often equal to snout length

Oblique, terminal mouth

Dark green or green-blue back

Silvery sides and silver-white belly

Ventral fins are pale grey; lighter than dorsal and tail fins

Short-based, grey dorsal fin with 7–9 rays

Deeply forked, grey tail fin

Moderately long-based, pale grey anal fin with 13–19 rays

Short, scaleless keel along belly between the pelvic fins and vent

Schneider *Alburnoides bipunctatus*

The schneider is a distinctively marked relative of the bleaks inhabiting clear streams and lakes where its shoals hug the bottom more than bleak. Because it is of little angling or economic value, its behaviour is not well known.

Distribution France eastwards through C Europe to Russia, but not mountainous areas nor Fenno-Scandia and N Russia, S to the Black Sea.

Habitat Clean streams with gravel or stone beds and some lakes.

Feeding Insect larvae and nymphs and crustaceans are taken from the river bed; schneider will also rise to take flies at the surface.

Size Maximum length 10-12cm; exceptionally 15cm.

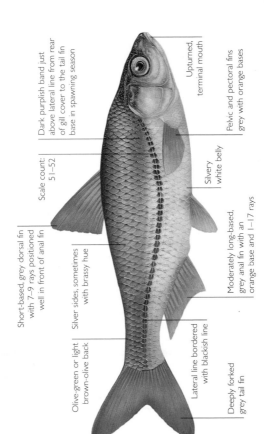

Dark purplish band just above lateral line from rear of gill cover to the tail fin base in spawning season

Upturned, terminal mouth

Scale count: 51-52

Pelvic and pectoral fins grey with orange bases

Silvery white belly

Short-based, grey dorsal fin with 7-9 rays positioned well in front of anal fin

Silver sides, sometimes with brassy hue

Moderately long-based, grey anal fin with an orange base and 1-17 rays

Olive-green or light brown-olive back

Lateral line bordered with blackish line

Deeply forked grey tail fin

Asp *Aspius aspius*

The asp is a streamlined, powerful predatory fish with the potential for growing to quite a large size for a cyprinid, and making it a popular angler's quarry. The second half of the 20th century saw a great decline of asp stocks so that it is now a fairly rare fish over much of its range.

Distribution NE Holland and N Germany eastwards through S Fenno-Scandia to Russia and S to rivers draining to the Black Sea.

Habitat Large river systems and lakes on them downstream to the estuary.

Feeding Juvenile asp are insect-eating shoal fish. Later they turn to a diet of lesser fish; they will also take amphibians and small birds such as moorhen chicks.

Size Maximum length about 60cm, weight 3.75kg; exceptionally to 1.2m, 12kg.

Fairly large head with pointed snout

Large mouth angled slightly upwards

Lower jaw extends slightly beyond upper jaw and has thick lip that fits into notch in upper jaw

Silvery sides

Dark olive-green back

White belly

Pectoral and pelvic fins deep red (pelvic fin has 8–9 rays)

Scale count: 65–74

Sharp keel in belly between pelvic fin and vent

Long-based, concave, deep red anal fin with pointed tips

Fairly short-based, slightly concave, dark grey-brown dorsal fin with pointed tips and 7–9 rays

Deeply forked dark grey-brown tail

Barbel *Barbus barbus*

This is the most widespread of several European species, the classification of which is far from settled. They take their name from the touch- and taste-sensitive barbels found at the underslung mouth: adaptations for feeding on a river bed. When folded back, the front barbels do not reach the nostrils. Powerful fish, they are highly popular amongst anglers.

Distribution W and C Europe, including SE England, E to Russia and the Black Sea; introduced to parts of W Britain. Absent from Ireland, Scotland and Fenno-Scandia.

Habitat Middle and lower reaches of clean rivers.

Feeding Riverbed invertebrates, including freshwater shrimp, insect larvae and nymphs, aquatic worms and snails.

Size Maximum length usually 60cm, weight 3kg; exceptionally to 90cm, 8.5kg.

Other similar species The Iberian barbel (*B. bocagei*) and Portuguese barbel (*B. comiza*) occur in the Iberian Peninsula; the Italian barbel (*B. plebejus*) appears in Italy and Slovenia.

Short-based, fairly long, pointed, dark brownish dorsal fin with long, serrated spine at front and 11–12 rays

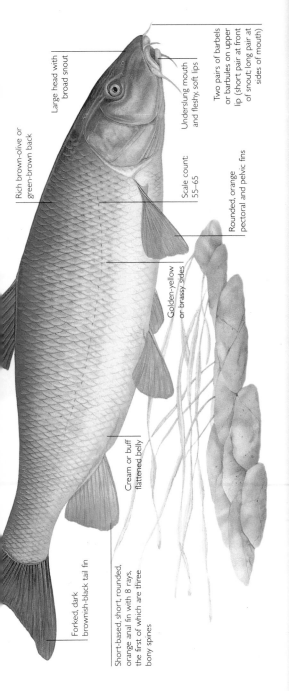

Large head with broad snout

Rich brown-olive or green-brown back

Underslung mouth and fleshy, soft lips

Two pairs of barbels or barbules on upper lip (short pair at front of snout; long pair at sides of mouth)

Scale count: 55–65

Rounded, orange pectoral and pelvic fins

Golden-yellow or brassy sides

Cream or buff flattened belly

Forked, dark brownish-black tail fin

Short-based, short, rounded, orange anal fin with 8 rays, the first of which are three bony spines

Mediterranean Barbel *Barbus meridionalis*

This southern-central European barbel is much smaller than the barbel (p 120-1) and for certain separation the front barbels, when folded back, reach the nostrils. The back coloration is usually more blotchy, and it tends to live in higher river reaches than the barbel.

Distribution C Iberia eastwards through S France and N Italy and Slovenia S to Greece and east through the Danube system.

Habitat Upper and middle reaches of rivers including shallow streams.

Feeding Invertebrates from the river bed, including caddis larvae, mayfly and stonefly nymphs, freshwater shrimps and aquatic snails.

Size Maximum length in range 20-25cm, weight about 800g.

Other related species The tiny Peloponnesian barbel (*B. peloponnesius*) of C Greece and countries bordering the E Adriatic is a close relation of the Mediterranean barbel.

Deeply forked, dark brown-black tail fin with light brown rays

Short-based, dark brown-black dorsal fin with 10–12 light brown rays – the first is a long, toothed bony spine and the next three are short spines

Scale count: 48–55

Large head with broad snout

Olive-brown back shading to lighter or yellow-olive brown sides

Short-based, rounded light buff anal fin with 8 rays – the first three are bony spines

Back and sides mottled with small blackish-brown spots

Light buff-brown or yellow-brown pelvic and pectoral fins

White flattened belly

Thick-lipped, underslung mouth bearing two pairs of barbels – one at front of snout, one at each side of mouth

Thracian Barbel *Barbus cyclolepis*

This species, restricted to rivers in SE Europe, can be separated from the other species (p 120–3) by its rounded belly and short barbels: when folded back the front pair reach only about halfway to the nostrils and the length of the rear pair equals eye diameter (longer in other barbels).

Distribution N Greece, Turkey and rivers draining to the S and E sides of the Black Sea.

Habitat Middle reaches of clean rivers.

Feeding Food taken from the river bed including midge and caddis larvae, mayfly and stonefly nymphs, snails and shrimps.

Size Maximum length in the range 20–25cm, weight about 500g; exceptionally over 30cm and 1kg.

Other similar species The Euboean barbel (*B. euboicus*) from the Greek island of Euboea and the Greek barbel (*B. graecus*) from the River Sperchios and lakes Paralimni and Yliki.

Large head with underslung mouth

Warm olive-brown back

Scale count: 49–55

Short-based, brown dorsal fin with long, pointed tips and 10–12 rays – the first is a long, toothed spine

Two pairs of short barbels (front pair is very short)

Pectoral and pelvic fins are light red-brown

White or cream rounded belly

Golden-olive sides

Short-based anal fin with long, pointed tips and 8 rays – the first three are bony spines

Gudgeon *Gobio gobio*

Superficially the gudgeon resembles a small barbel, but instead of having two pairs of barbels at the mouth the gudgeon has only one pair, each of which has a length less than two times eye diameter. It is a bottom-feeding fish, rarely straying to mid-water.

Distribution Cantabrian Mountains and Pyrenees (Spain) eastwards through France and SE Britain to Asia, but not N Fenno-Scandia, Italy and countries bordering the Adriatic. Introduced W Britain and Ireland.

Habitat Clean rivers, lakes and canals.

Feeding Mostly larvae, pupae and nymphs of aquatic insects; also freshwater shrimps and snails.

Size Maximum length 8-10cm; exceptionally to 20cm.

Deeply forked, light brown tail fin with dark blotches

Green- or olive-brown back

Short-based, light brown dorsal fin with dark blotches and 9–11 rays

Silvery sides with strong yellow hue and series of dark, rounded blotches

Short-based, light brown anal fin with dark blotches and 7–9 rays

Silver-white belly

Warm creamy buff or orange-buff pectoral and pelvic fins with no spotting

Scale count: 38–44

Throat scaleless

Fleshy lips with one barbel at each corner

Large head with ventral mouth

White-finned Gudgeon *Gobio albipinnatus*

The fins of white-finned gudgeon are not white but a pale olive or brown-olive; they are, however, unmarked. The barbels are much longer than in the gudgeon: 2–3 times eye diameter. This tiny fish occurs only in SE Europe.

Distribution Lower reaches of the Danube and other rivers flowing to the Black and Caspian Seas.

Habitat Slow-flowing silty-bottomed rivers.

Feeding Mainly midge larvae and pupae that are taken from the river bed, but other aquatic invertebrates may feature.

Size Maximum length in range 10–12cm.

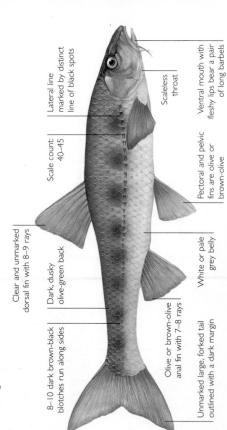

Lateral line marked by distinct line of black spots

Scaleless throat

Scale count: 40–45

Ventral mouth with fleshy lips bear a pair of long barbels

Pectoral and pelvic fins are olive or brown-olive

Clear and unmarked dorsal fin with 8–9 rays

Dark, dusky olive-green back

8–10 dark brown-black blotches run along sides

White or pale grey belly

Olive or brown-olive anal fin with 7–8 rays

Unmarked large, forked tail outlined with a dark margin

Kessler's Gudgeon *Gobio kessleri*

Kessler's gudgeon has long barbels (2–3 times eye diameter), belly as well as throat scaleless, and the dorsal and tail fins have dark markings. A fish of fast-flowing rocky streams in C Europe and, because it is nocturnal, easily overlooked.

Distribution Tributaries of the upper and middle reaches of the Rivers Danube and Dnestr.

Habitat Rocky, fast-flowing clean streams.

Feeding A bottom-feeder on small river bed invertebrates including mayfly and stonefly nymphs, caddis and small snails.

Size Maximum length mostly in range 8–11 cm.

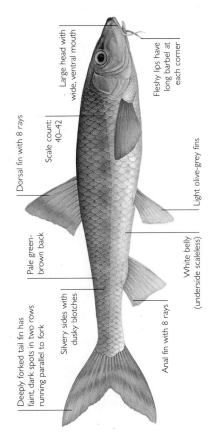

Large head with wide, ventral mouth

Dorsal fin with 8 rays

Scale count: 40–42

Fleshy lips have long barbel at each corner

Light olive-grey fins

Deeply forked tail fin has faint, dark spots in two rows running parallel to fork

Pale green-brown back

Silvery sides with dusky blotches

Anal fin with 8 rays

White belly (underside scaleless)

Danube Gudgeon *Gobio uranoscopus*

Found only in the Danube system, this species resembles Kessler's gudgeon (p 129), with barbel length 2-3 times eye diameter and dark markings on tail and dorsal fins; but the entire body is scaled. Easily overlooked because it is nocturnal.

Distribution Upper tributaries of River Danube.

Habitat Fast, turbulent rocky rivers.

Feeding Bottom-feeder on river bed invertebrates including mayfly and stonefly nymphs, small snails etc.

Size Maximum length 12cm.

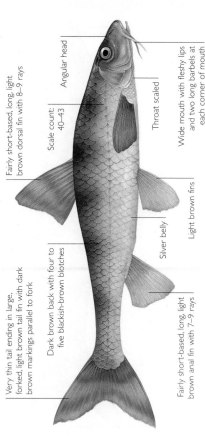

Fairly short-based, long, light brown dorsal fin with 8-9 rays

Angular head

Scale count: 40-43

Throat scaled

Wide mouth with fleshy lips and two long barbels at each corner of mouth

Light brown fins

Silver belly

Very thin tail ending in large, forked, light brown tail fin with dark brown markings parallel to fork

Dark brown back with four to five blackish-brown blotches

Fairly short-based, long, light brown anal fin with 7-9 rays

Barbel-Gudgeon *Aulopyge hugeli*

This tiny fish resembles a scaleless gudgeon with, like the barbels, two pairs of barbels. Little is known of the fish because of its often hidden habitat in a fairly remote corner of SE Europe.

Distribution Dalmatia, Bosnia and Herzegovina.

Habitat Mountain rivers (and lakes), including underground streams.

Feeding A bottom-feeder rarely straying to mid-water. Invertebrate foods include mayfly and stonefly nymphs, midge larvae, small snails and crustaceans.

Size Maximum length in the range 10-13cm.

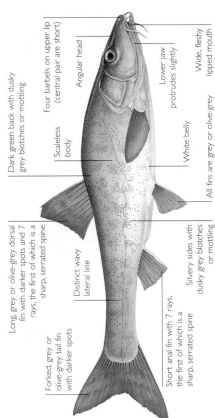

Dark green back with dusky grey blotches or mottling

Four barbels on upper lip (central pair are short)

Angular head

Scaleless body

Lower jaw protrudes slightly

White belly

Wide, fleshy lipped mouth

All fins are grey or olive-grey

Long, grey or olive-grey dorsal fin with darker spots and 7 rays, the first of which is a sharp, serrated spine

Forked, grey or olive-grey tail fin with darker spots

Distinct wavy lateral line

Short anal fin with 7 rays, the first of which is a sharp, serrated spine

Silvery sides with dusky grey blotches or mottling

Tench *Tinca tinca*

A favourite amongst anglers, the tench is a summer fish, hibernating through the winter. Its stout powerful build and rounded fins, olive coloration (there is a rare golden form) and small red eyes prevent confusion with any other European fish. A fish of murky, weedy meres.

Distribution Throughout much of Europe except N Scotland, Iceland, N Fenno-Scandia and Russia and countries bordering the E Adriatic. Introduced to Ireland and W Britain.

Habitat Lowland lakes and canals.

Feeding Almost all food is taken from the bottom, where it grubs in mud and silt for invertebrates such as midge larvae and water hog-lice. Feeding tench located by masses of tiny bubbles at the water surface.

Size Maximum length about 50cm, weight 2kg; exceptionally to 8kg.

Yellow-olive, bronze or olive-brown sides

Body covered with tiny scales glazed with transparent mucus

Short, broad head

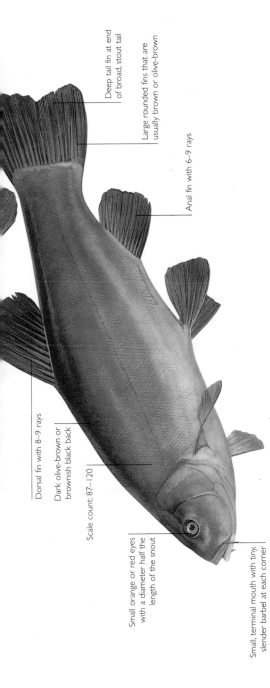

Deep tail fin at end of broad, stout tail

Large rounded fins that are usually brown or olive-brown

Anal fin with 6–9 rays

Dorsal fin with 8–9 rays

Dark olive-brown or brownish black back

Scale count: 87–120

Small orange or red eyes with a diameter half the length of the snout

Small, terminal mouth with tiny, slender barbel at each corner

Nase *Chondrostoma nasus*

The seven species of European nase are unique amongst cyprinids in that they feed by grazing algae from rocks using a rasp-like lower lip. The nase is the commonest and most widespread species, with three very similar, closely related species.

Distribution France eastwards through C Europe to Russia (not N Europe nor extreme S).

Habitat Middle and upper river reaches with boulder or bedrock bed.

Feeding A shoal fish that grazes algae (diatoms and filamentous green) from rocks. It probably ingests some animal matter with the algae. Has been reported taking some invertebrates.

Size Maximum length is usually about 40cm; exceptionally 50cm.

Other similar species The Iberian nase (*C. polylepis*) replaces the nase in Spain and Portugal, the lasca nase (*C. genei*) in N and C Italy, and the savetta nase (*C. soetta*) in the Italian River Po system.

Deeply forked, dark grey tail fin with rounded tips

Short-based dark grey dorsal fin with 9-13 rays; base slightly in front of pelvic bases

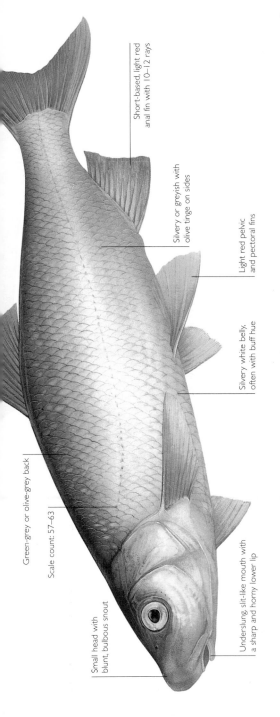

Short-based, light red anal fin with 10–12 rays

Silvery or greyish with olive tinge on sides

Light red pelvic and pectoral fins

Silvery white belly, often with buff hue

Green-grey or olive-grey back

Scale count: 57–63

Small head with blunt, bulbous snout

Underslung, slit-like mouth with a sharp and horny lower lip

Southwest European Nase (or Soiffe) *Chondrostoma toxostoma*

This species superficially resembles the nase, but the mouth is more curved to a horseshoe shape, the fins are yellow and the dorsal fin base is in line with the pelvic bases. Like the other nases it has a specialised feeding system.

Distribution C Spain, the Pyrenees and SE France.

Habitat Upper and middle stretches of rocky rivers; also some mountain lakes.

Feeding Scrapes algae from rocks with its lower lip; feeds in shoals.

Size Maximum length 20-25cm; exceptionally to 30cm.

Other similar species The Dalmatian nase (*C. knieri*) is found in rivers draining to the Dalmatian coast.

Dark grey-yellow tail fin

Dark blue- or olive-green back

Short-based dark grey-yellow dorsal fin with 9 rays; base in line with pelvic fin bases.

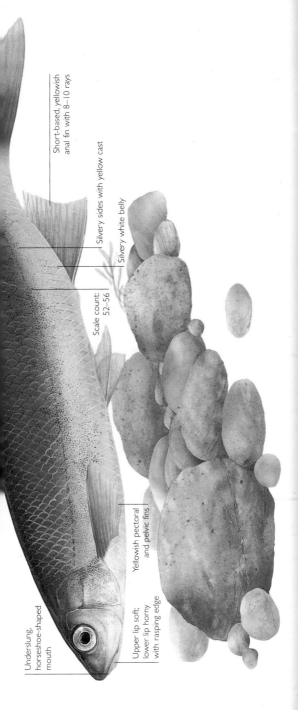

Undersling, horseshoe-shaped mouth

Upper lip soft; lower lip horny with rasping edge

Yellowish pectoral and pelvic fins

Scale count: 52–56

Silvery white belly

Silvery sides with yellow cast

Short-based, yellowish anal fin with 8–10 rays

Minnow Nase *Chondrostoma phoxinus*

The yellow fins and horseshoe-shaped mouth might result in the minnow nase being mistaken for the southwest European nase (p 136-7), but its much larger lateral line scale count, tiny size and isolated distribution prevent this. It too is a specialist feeder on algae.

Feeding Feeds on algae that it scrapes from rock with its hard-edged lower lip.

Size Average length 6cm; maximum to 8cm.

Distribution Rivers draining to the Dalmatian coast.

Habitat Shallow streamy pools and riffles with a bedrock or boulder bed.

Forked, dark brown tail fin with rounded tips

Short-based, dark brown dorsal fin with 11 rays

Scale count: 85-90

Pointed snout (but not as bulbous as other nase species)

Yellowish band in front of tail fin

Short-based, drab yellow anal fin with 10–11 rays

Dark olive-brown back

Silvery sides with copper or bronze sheen

Silvery white belly

Drab yellow pectoral and pelvic fins

Horseshoe-shaped underslung mouth

Soft, fleshy upper lip; hard, sharp-edged lower lip

Identifying cyprinid hybrids

Cyprinids usually spawn in shoals, with different species often sharing the same parts of rivers or lakes. The females shed their eggs and the males release clouds of sperm that drift in the water over the eggs, fertilising them. Consequently it is not unusual for the sperm of one species to fertilise the eggs of another, especially where populations are huge. For instance, in many lakes and rivers in Ireland, where bream, roach and rudd are very abundant, bream x roach, bream x rudd and roach x rudd hybrids are common.

Hybrids usually show characters of both parent species, or characters that are somewhere between those of the two parents : Roach x bream hybrid (see pp 92-3 and 104-5 for parent species).

The following are amongst the commonest hybrids:

Roach x bream, Roach x bleak, Roach x silver bream, Roach x rudd, Carp x crucian carp, Rudd x dace, Rudd x bream, Rudd x silver bream, Rudd x bleak, Bream x silver bream, Bleak x chub, Bleak x dace, Bleak x silver bream

Shown here Roach x bream hybrid

Eye diameter approximately equal to snout length

Similar mouth to the roach

Blue-grey or grey-brown back, deeper than that of the roach

Dorsal fin with 9 rays

Light brown pelvic and pectoral fins often with a red cast

Silvery sides often with dull copper or brownish cast

Slimy body as in bream

Anal fin with 15–20 rays (midway between roach and bream ray counts)

Details of identification of the commoner hybrids can be found in *Freshwater Fish* p 141

Stone Loach Noemacheilus (Barbatula) barbatula

Loaches are small, slender bottom-feeding fish that always have more than two pairs of barbels around the mouth. Stone loach are often overlooked because they are mainly nocturnal, hiding away by day, and are well camouflaged.

Distribution Pyrenees and SE Britain eastwards through C Europe to Russia; introduced W Britain and Ireland.

Habitat Clean rivers and lakes; usually those that are boulder-bottomed.

Feeding Fairly solitary feeders on microscopic algae and tiny crustaceans and small insect larvae and pupae.

Size Maximum in range 8-12cm; exceptionally to 15cm.

Shallow-forked, buff-yellow tail fin with dark spotting and rounded corners

Short-based yellow-buff anal fin with dark spotting and 7–10 rays, midway between pelvics and tail fin

Brown-olive or dirty yellow-brown back

Short-based, yellow-buff dorsal fin with dark spotting and 9–11 rays

Pelvic fins opposite dorsal and midway down body

Pale yellow body covered with slime

Light yellow-brown sides with irregular dark grey-brown blotches

Dark spots on yellow-buff pelvic and pectoral fins

Scales small, lateral line visible at front only

Underslung mouth has six barbels (four in front; two at corners)

Fairly small head

Pond Loach (Weatherfish) *Misgurnus fossilis*

A fish of small pools with low oxygen levels, the name 'weatherfish' comes from the behaviour of the fish to swim to the surface to gulp air when hot thundery weather sets in. It will also burrow in the mud bed to aestivate during hot droughts.

Distribution C France eastwards (not British Isles) through C Europe to Russia.

Habitat Ponds and weedy meres.

Feeding Nocturnal feeder on midge larvae, water hog-lice and other small aquatic invertebrates.

Size Length usually in the range 12–25cm; exceptionally to 35cm.

Light yellow-brown fins with darker patches that sometimes form bands, particularly on the tail fin

Lines or stripes break up into spots along tail

Drab brown or yellow-brown back shading to sandy sides

Small rounded anal fin with 5–6 rays nearer pelvic fins than tail fin

Short-based dorsal fin with 5–7 rays

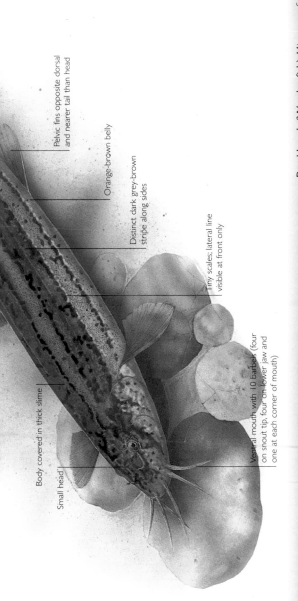

Pelvic fins opposite dorsal and nearer tail than head

Orange-brown belly

Distinct dark grey-brown stripe along sides

Tiny scales; lateral line visible at front only

Ventral mouth with 10 barbels (four on snout tip, four on lower jaw and one at each corner of mouth)

Body covered in thick slime

Small head

Spined Loach *Cobitis taenia*

Nocturnal, burrowing in mud during the day, so easily overlooked, the spined loach lives in stagnant water and can gulp air from the surface when oxygen levels fall. The tiny spine which gives the fish its name can be felt by gently stroking the side of the head just below the eyes.

Distribution Throughout Europe except for Iceland, Ireland, NW Britain, most of Fenno-Scandia and N Russia and S Greece.

Habitat Canals, lakes and very sluggish rivers.

Feeding Most foods taken by filtering mud and ingesting whatever is living in the mud; also will select small invertebrates.

Size Average length 5cm; exceptionally to 10-12cm.

Other similar species Spanish populations have been separated into *C. calderoni* (N Spain) and *C. maroccana* (S Spain). Romanian population named as *Sabanejewia romanica*, Italian population *S. larvata*. Balkan loach (*C. elongata*) from Balkan rivers and golden loach (*C. aurata*) from Danube.

Short-based, pale yellow-buff dorsal fin with 7-10 rays

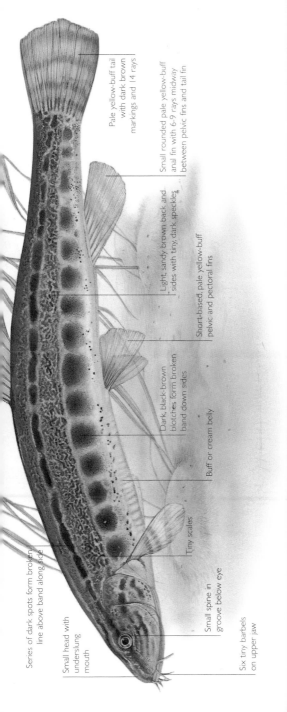

Pale yellow-buff tail with dark brown markings and 14 rays

Small rounded pale yellow-buff anal fin with 6-9 rays midway between pelvic fins and tail fin

Light, sandy brown back and sides with tiny, dark speckles

Short-based, pale yellow-buff pelvic and pectoral fins

Dark, black-brown blotches form broken band down sides

Buff or cream belly

Series of dark spots form broken line above band along side

Tiny scales

Small head with underslung mouth

Small spine in groove below eye

Six tiny barbels on upper jaw

European Catfish (or Wels) *Siluris glanis*

This catfish is the largest resident freshwater fish in Europe (sturgeon migrate to sea). It is a powerful solitary nocturnal predator and such a popular anglers' fish that it has been introduced to many areas where it is not native. A warm-water species, it hibernates in winter.

Distribution E Germany and Poland eastwards through E Europe, but not N Europe nor S of Alps; introduced to W Germany, France, Spain and England.

Habitat Lakes and deep lowland rivers.

Feeding Mainly lesser fish, but has been recorded taking waterfowl and amphibious mammals.

Size Slow-growing, 2-10kg at 10 years, but after 15-20 years up to 200kg; exceptionally to 306kg.

Two long, slender barbels on upper jaw

Tiny brown-black or blue-black dorsal fin with 3-5 rays

Slimy, scaleless skin

Pale patches on back and darker patches on sides give marbled appearance

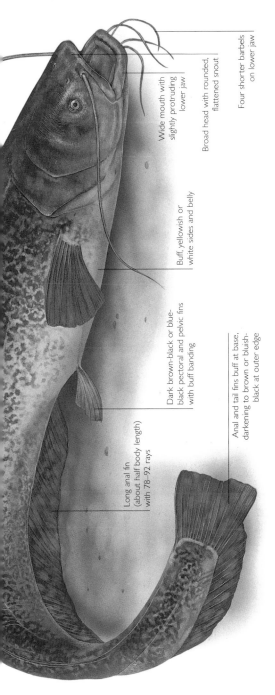

Wide mouth with slightly protruding lower jaw

Broad head with rounded, flattened snout

Four shorter barbels on lower jaw

Buff, yellowish or white sides and belly

Dark brown-black or blue-black pectoral and pelvic fins with buff banding

Long anal fin (about half body length) with 78–92 rays

Anal and tail fins buff at base, darkening to brown or bluish-black at outer edge

Aristotle's Catfish *Siluris aristotelis*

Smaller than the European catfish (p 148-9), this species has only two pairs of barbels and has a restricted range in Greece. Solitary fish, they are most active between dusk and dawn and take smaller prey than the European catfish.

Distribution River Akheloos and Lakes Amvrakia, Azeros, Jannina, Lyssimakhia, Trikhonis and Volvi.

Habitat Lakes and deep slow rivers.

Feeding Large invertebrates, amphibians and lesser fish.

Size Length in range 0.4-1m; exceptionally to 1.5m.

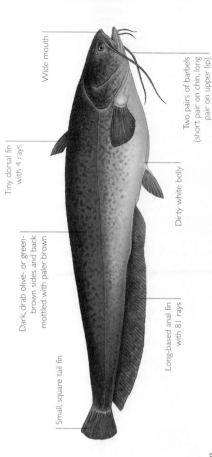

Wide mouth

Tiny dorsal fin with 4 rays

Dark drab olive- or green-brown sides and back mottled with paler brown

Two pairs of barbels (short pair on chin, long pair on upper lip)

Dirty white belly

Small, square tail fin

Long-based anal fin with 81 rays

Black Bullhead *Ictalurus melas*

Introduced from North America, this species seems slowly to be spreading through the warmer waters of Europe. It has been confused with small specimens of the European catfish, but has four pairs of barbels and more typical fin arrangement.

Distribution C and S Europe from France eastwards.

Habitat Lowland lakes, ponds, canals; slow rivers.

Feeding A nocturnal bottom-feeder on larger invertebrates and eggs and fry of other fish.

Size Usually reaches 30–35cm in Europe; up to 70cm in N America.

Other similar species The similar brown bullhead (*I. nebulosus*) has also been introduced to Europe, but is less widespread.

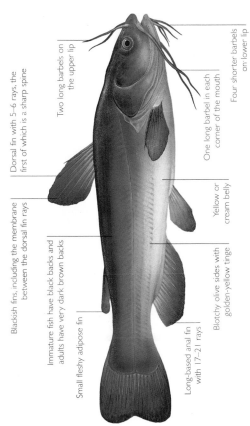

Dorsal fin with 5–6 rays, the first of which is a sharp spine

Two long barbels on the upper lip

Blackish fins, including the membrane between the dorsal fin rays

Immature fish have black backs and adults have very dark brown backs

One long barbel in each corner of the mouth

Small fleshy adipose fin

Yellow or cream belly

Four shorter barbels on lower lip

Long-based anal fin with 17–21 rays

Blotchy olive sides with golden-yellow tinge

Burbot *Lota lota*

The only freshwater member of the cod family, the burbot is highly regarded as a food in some parts of Europe, especially the liver which contains vitamin A- and D-rich oil. They are mainly nocturnal through the summer, but feed actively by day in the coldest winter conditions.

Distribution Eastern France eastwards, except for the far S. Extinct in Britain.

Habitat Clean lowland lakes and large slow rivers.

Feeding Larger invertebrates (e.g. opossum shrimp, freshwater mussels, insect larvae) and lesser fish that are taken both from the bottom and from mid-water.

Size Maximum length about 50cm, weight about 1kg; maximum 1.2m.

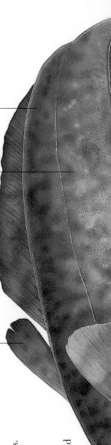

Overall coloration sandy, yellow-olive or medium brown

Dark brown blotches concentrated on back

Two dorsal fins – short front one with 10–14 rays and long rear one with 60–80 rays

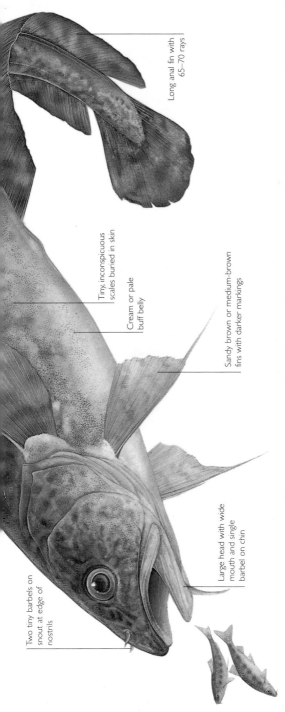

Two tiny barbels on snout at edge of nostrils

Tiny, inconspicuous scales buried in skin

Cream or pale buff belly

Long anal fin with 65–70 rays

Sandy brown or medium-brown fins with darker markings

Large head with wide mouth and single barbel on chin

Spanish Toothcarp *Aphanius iberus*

A tiny fish of shallow, brackish coastal pools. Development of coastal areas is destroying the habitat of the Spanish toothcarp. Introduced American mosquito fish are competing successfully with this European fish.

Distribution Spain's Mediterranean coastal fringes.

Habitat Shallow, weedy, stagnant meres, lagoons and ditches.

Feeding A mid-water and surface feeder on planktonic crustaceans and midge and mosquito larvae and pupae.

Size Maximum length 5-6cm.

Shown here Female

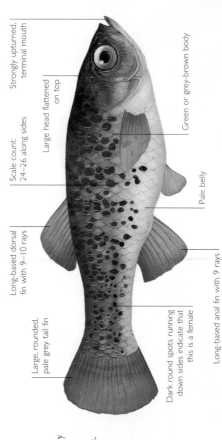

Strongly upturned, terminal mouth

Large head flattened on top

Green or grey-brown body

Scale count: 24–26 along sides

Pale belly

Long-based dorsal fin with 9–10 rays

Large, rounded, pale grey tail fin

Dark round spots running down sides indicate that this is a female

Long-based anal fin with 9 rays

Mediterranean Toothcarp *Aphanius fasciatus*

This small stumpy fish is found in coastal pools around the Mediterranean coastline. Development of this coastline is increasingly destroying Mediterranean toothcarp habitat. The strongly upturned mouth indicates a feeder in mid-water and the surface.

Distribution Mediterranean coastal fringes, including islands except the Balearics.

Habitat Brackish weedy pools, swamps and ditches.

Feeding Planktonic crustaceans, and midge and mosquito larvae, pupae and some adult flies.

Size Maximum length 4-6cm.

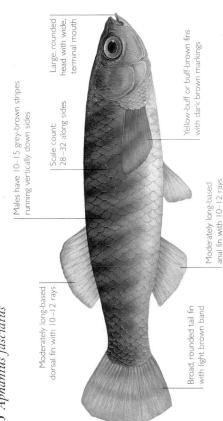

Males have 10–15 grey-brown stripes running vertically down sides

Large, rounded head with wide, terminal mouth

Scale count: 28–32 along sides

Yellow-buff or buff-brown fins with dark brown markings

Moderately long-based dorsal fin with 10–12 rays

Moderately long-based anal fin with 10–12 rays

Broad, rounded tail fin with light brown band

Three-spined Stickleback *Gasterosteus aculeatus*

This tiny spiny fish is amongst the best known. Some populations migrate to sea to feed and are silvery on their return. Although three-spined sticklebacks are scaleless, some populations have bony plates along the sides.

Distribution Throughout much of Europe other than inland mountainous areas.

Habitat Slow rivers, canals, lakes and small ponds; also clean estuaries.

Feeding Invertebrates, including planktonic crustaceans, insect larvae, small snails and worms.

Size Maximum length 5-8cm; to 11cm in sea-going specimens.

Shown here Female laying eggs (bottom), male guarding nest.

Thin tail with fan-shaped tail fin

Olive-green to blue-black back

Long-based anal fin with 1 spine + 8 rays

Silvery sides with dark blackish speckling

Long-based dorsal fin with 10–12 rays

Three, occasionally two, sharp spines on back in front of dorsal fin

Large distinct pectoral fins with blue, yellow or olive hue

Red throat

Females and non-breeding males lack the red throat.

Large head with slightly upturned mouth and protruding lower lip

Nine-spined Stickleback (*Pungitius pungitius*)

One of the tiniest European fish, the nine-spined stickleback is often overlooked. It lives in water that, in summer, has such low oxygen levels that most other fish are unable to survive. The black on the male's throat develops only in the breeding season.

Distribution N Europe from Ireland and S Britain and N France eastwards, but not Iceland, N Scotland and W Norway.

Habitat Weed-choked ponds, lake margins and river backwaters.

Feeding Mainly planktonic crustaceans and midge and mosquito larvae and pupae.

Size Maximum about 5cm; exceptionally to 7cm.

Shown here Spawning male (top), female/non-breeder (bottom).

Long-based dorsal fin with 9–12 rays

Very slender tail

Fan-shaped tail fin

Dark bluish-green to brown back and sides

Black throat

Body scaleless

Short spine at front of long-based anal fin with I spine + 9–11 rays

Pale belly, sometimes silvery white

Pelvic fins are just two short spines

VIII–XII (usually IX, often X, rarely VIII, XI or XII) short, slender spines along back

Large head with pointed snout

Terminal mouth with slightly protruding lower lip

Miller's Thumb (or Sculpin) *Cottus gobio*

A characteristic fish of small, clean, boulder-strewn rivers, the miller's thumb is often overlooked because it is nocturnal, hiding away during the day. Through spring, clumps of large yellow eggs, stuck to the underside of boulders, often betray the presence of large unseen populations.

Distribution N Spain eastwards through C and N Europe; not N Scotland or Ireland.

Habitat Clean rivers and lakes, usually with boulder beds.

Feeding Mainly invertebrates, including mayfly and stonefly nymphs, caddis larvae, worms, freshwater shrimps and fish eggs and newly hatched fry.

Size Maximum about 10cm; exceptionally to 16cm.

Light sandy brown, green-brown or medium brown back mottled with dark brown

Two dorsal fins joined by fine membrane with VI–IX spines + 15–18 rays

Long-based anal fin with 12–13 rays

Pale cream belly

Huge pectoral fins

Line of up to 35 pores details lateral line along each side

Big eyes positioned on top of head

Large, flattened head

Light sandy brown fins with dark spotting on rays that can look like stripes

Bass (or Sea Bass) *Dicentrarchus labrax*

Although primarily a sea fish, this shoaling predator (the French call it, 'wolf of the sea') penetrates as far as the limits of freshwater in estuaries during summer. A gourmet's delight and popular sport-fish, bass are not farmed in the Mediterranean. It is the most spiny of European fish: Beware!

Distribution Coastal areas from S Norway and Denmark S, including the British Isles (not N Scotland and Iceland) to the Mediterranean.

Habitat Inshore waters including estuaries.

Feeding Voracious hunter of lesser fish, including sand-eels, and larger crustaceans including crabs and shrimps.

Size Mostly maximum length 35-40cm, weighing about 1.5kg; exceptionally 5-9kg.

Other similar species Spotted bass (*D. punctatus*) along the coasts from S France to the W Mediterranean.

Two separate dorsal fins; front has VIII–IX spines and rear has 1 spine + 12–13 rays

Steel-grey back with green or olive tinge

Anal fin bears III strong, sharp spines and 10–12 rays

Bright silver sides

Scale count: 52–74

Silvery white belly

Grey fins

Spines at rear edge of gill cover

Bulky head with large, conspicuous eyes

Wide mouth

Largemouth Bass *Micropterus salmoides*

This and the smallmouth bass were introduced from N America for their hard-fighting quality. Both require very warm water for breeding, and so it is unlikely that they will become established through N Europe.

Distribution Introduced to S England, France, Belgium, Holland and Germany.

Habitat Lakes and canals: will spawn only in very warm water.

Feeding Lesser fish, amphibians and large invertebrates which it ambushes from cover.

Size Maximum length 40-50cm; occasionally to 80cm.

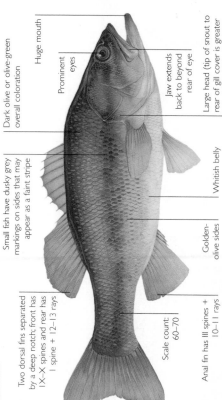

Dark olive or olive-green overall coloration

Huge mouth

Prominent eyes

Jaw extends back to beyond rear of eye

Large head (tip of snout to rear of gill cover is greater than depth of body)

Small fish have dusky grey markings on sides that may appear as a faint stripe

Two dorsal fins separated by a deep notch; front has IX–X spines and rear has I spine + 12–13 rays

Whitish belly

Golden-olive sides

Scale count: 60–70

Anal fin has III spines + 10–11 rays

Smallmouth Bass *Micropterus dolomieu*

Easy separation from the closely related largemouth bass is based on jaw length, the depth of notch between the two dorsal fins and, in this species, vertical barring down the body. Introduced from North America.

Distribution Reported introductions to Jutland, S Finland, N France and Belgium, but needs very warm water for spawning.

Habitat Lakes; preferably open water.

Feeding A predator, taking lesser fish, amphibians and larger invertebrates.

Size Usual length 30–35cm, exceptionally to 50cm

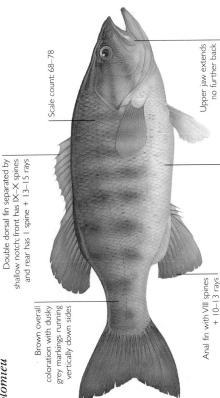

Double dorsal fin separated by shallow notch; front has IX–X spines and rear has 1 spine + 13–15 rays

Scale count: 68–78

Upper jaw extends no further back than rear of eye

Whitish belly

Brown overall coloration with dusky grey markings running vertically down the sides

Anal fin with VIII spines + 10–13 rays

Perch *Perca fluviatilis*

One of the best-known European fish. Some lakes may have huge shoals of tiny fish, whilst others have smaller populations of much larger fish. In recent years 'perch disease' has almost wiped out the stocks from many lakes; the real cause is unknown.

Distribution Most of Europe (other than the far N and far S) east of the Pyrenees.

Habitat Lakes, canals and slower rivers.

Feeding Smaller perch feed mainly on invertebrates, but larger ones will hunt smaller fish including tiny perch.

Size Maximum length 30–35cm; weight about 1.5kg; exceptionally larger.

Large dark olive-brown dorsal fin; front part has XIII–XVII spines and rear part has I–II spines + 13–17 rays

Dark olive-brown back

Four to six obvious blackish bars running down sides

Anal fin supported by 11 long, sharp spines + 8–10 rays

White or cream belly

Bright orange or red pelvic, anal and tail fins

Scale count: 58–68

Light olive or golden-olive sides

Drab olive-brown pectoral fins supported by long, sharp spines as well as rays

Rear of gill cover terminates in flat, sharp spine

Small, triangular head

Short snout and large mouth

Ruffe (or Pope) *Gymnocephalus cernuus*

This is the most widespread of the five European species of ruffe, very small, mainly bottom-living fish. Although they feed mainly on invertebrates, they will also attack tiny fish. Anglers have introduced the ruffe to some areas where it did not occur naturally.

Distribution SE Britain and NE France eastwards through C and N Europe (not Iceland and W Scandinavia); introduced to most of Britain (not Ireland) and most of N and C France.

Habitat Slower rivers, canals and lakes.

Feeding Insects such as caddis, water hog-lice, snails and midge larvae); also the eggs and fry of other fish.

Size Maximum length usually 10-15cm.

Two dorsal fins clearly joined; front is supported by XI–XVI spines and rear by 11–16 rays

Dark sandy brown to olive-brown back

Dark brown flecks on dorsal and tail fins

Scale count: 35–40

Short, triangular head and large mouth

Gill cover ends in flat, sharp spine

Pale buff-brown or sandy yellow fins

Pale cream or buff belly

Sandy or yellow-brown sides

Sides and back have dark brown blotches and speckles

Short-based anal fin; II spines + 5–6 rays

Striped Ruffe *Gymnocephalus schraetzer*

A Danubian species that can be easily separated from the ruffe by the stripes running along the body. It is a bottom-feeder, and tends to be nocturnal, spending the day resting in deep water.

Distribution River Danube system.

Habitat Slow deep pools and back-waters, with sand or gravel bed.

Feeding Mainly invertebrates: caddis, midge larvae and pupae, crustaceans, snails, worms etc. It will also take fry and eggs of other fish.

Size Maximum length 15–20cm; occasionally to 25cm.

Other related species Don ruffe (*G. acerina*) occur in rivers draining into the N of the Black Sea.

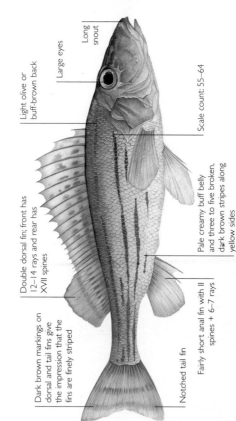

Light olive or buff-brown back

Long snout

Large eyes

Double dorsal fin; front has 12–14 rays and rear has XVII spines

Dark brown markings on dorsal and tail fins give the impression that the fins are finely striped

Scale count: 55–64

Pale creamy buff belly and three to five broken, dark brown stripes along yellow sides

Notched tail fin

Fairly short anal fin with II spines + 6–7 rays

Balon's Ruffe *Gymnocephalus baloni*

This very small Danubian ruffe can be separated from other ruffe species by the dark brown spotting, concentrated to give 4–6 bands along the body. A shoaling bottom-feeder; mainly nocturnal.

Distribution River Danube system.

Habitat Deep, slow, mud- or silt-bottomed pools.

Feeding Invertebrates, including insect larvae and small crustaceans; it may also eat fish eggs and fry.

Size Maximum length about 10cm.

Other related species Black Sea Ruffe (*Percarina demidoffi*) occurs in rivers draining to the Black Sea.

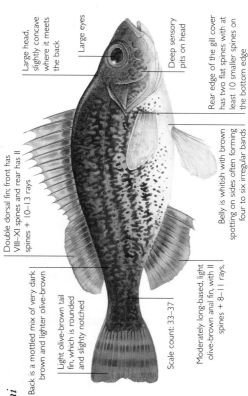

Large head, slightly concave where it meets the back

Large eyes

Deep sensory pits on head

Double dorsal fin; front has VIII–XI spines and rear has II spines + 10–13 rays

Rear edge of the gill cover has two flat spines with at least 10 smaller spines on the bottom edge

Back is a mottled mix of very dark brown and lighter olive-brown

Belly is whitish with brown spotting on sides often forming four to six irregular bands

Light olive-brown tail fin, which is rounded and slighty notched

Scale count: 33–37

Moderately long-based, light olive-brown anal fin, with II spines + 8–11 rays,

Zander (or Pike-Perch) *Stizostedion lucioperca*

The zander is a member of the perch family but with a predatory feeding behaviour reminiscent of the pike. A popular anglers' quarry and native of C and E Europe, it has been introduced to W Europe. Its eyes sometimes appear opaque: this is an adaptation to seeing in murky water.

Distribution NE France eastwards through C Europe and into Russia. Introduced to C and W France and England.

Habitat Lower slow river reaches, lakes and canals.

Feeding Lesser fish. The zander feeds well in murky water, and in clear water tends to be a crepuscular feeder.

Size Maximum length 0.9–1.1m, weight 5–7kg.

Other similar species Volga zander (*S. volgensis*) occur in lakes and rivers draining to the Black and N Caspian Seas.

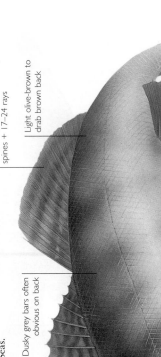

Double dark grey-brown dorsal fin clearly separated; front supported by XIII–XVII long, sharp spines and rear by II spines + 17–24 rays

Light olive-brown to drab brown back

Dusky grey bars often obvious on back

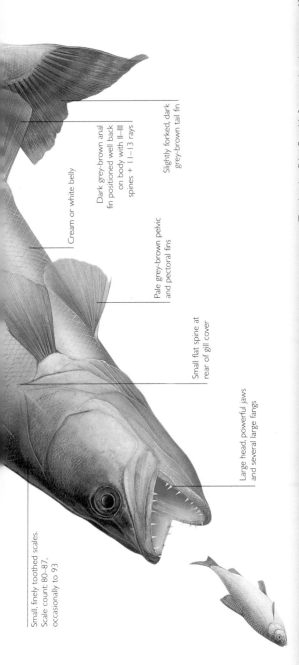

Small, finely toothed scales. Scale count: 80–87, occasionally to 93

Cream or white belly

Dark grey-brown anal fin positioned well back on body with II–III spines + 11–13 rays

Slightly forked, dark grey-brown tail fin

Pale grey-brown pelvic and pectoral fins

Small flat spine at rear of gill cover

Large head, powerful jaws and several large fangs

Asper Zingel (Aspro) asper

A very rare, small zander-like fish which can be separated from other similar members of the Perch family by the sizes and relative positions of dorsal and anal fins and shape of the snout. The asper occurs in only one river.

Distribution River Rhône.

Habitat Upper and middle river reaches.

Feeding A crepuscular or nocturnal feeder on mayfly and stonefly nymphs, caddis, freshwater shrimps and snails.

Size Maximum length about 15cm.

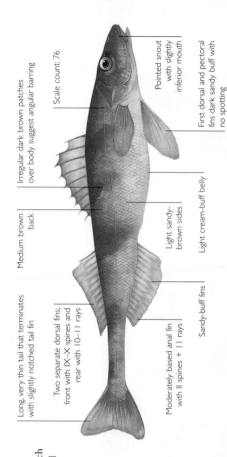

Scale count: 76

Irregular dark brown patches over body suggest angular barring

Pointed snout with slightly inferior mouth

First dorsal and pectoral fins dark sandy buff with no spotting

Medium brown back

Light sandy-brown sides

Light cream-buff belly

Long, very thin tail that terminates with slightly notched tail fin

Two separate dorsal fins; front with IX–X spines and rear with 10–11 rays

Moderately based anal fin with II spines + 11 rays

Sandy-buff fins

Asprete *Romanichthys valsanicola*

A small, slender relative of the zander, the asprete was discovered as recently as 1957 in three Romanian rivers. It is possible that it is extinct in two of these and rare in the third.

Distribution Rivers Argesul, Riul Doamnei and Vislan, tributaries of the R Arges in Romania.

Habitat Fast, turbulent clean rivers.

Feeding Not well known. Mayfly and stonefly nymphs and caddis probably predominant.

Size Maximum length about 12cm.

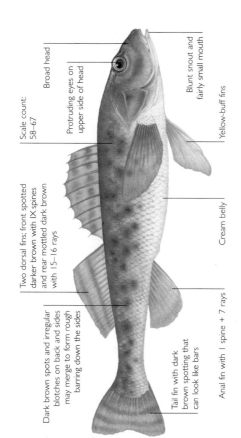

Scale count: 58–67

Broad head

Protruding eyes on upper side of head

Two dorsal fins; front spotted darker brown with IX spines and rear mottled dark brown with 15–16 rays

Dark brown spots and irregular blotches on back and sides may merge to form rough barring down the sides

Blunt snout and fairly small mouth

Yellow-buff fins

Cream belly

Tail fin with dark brown spotting that can look like bars

Anal fin with I spine + 7 rays

Streber Zingel (Aspro) streber

With the zingel, the streber is one of two small zander-like fish of the Danube system. This is the more slender one, with a long thin tail; it also tends to occur in smaller tributaries than the zingel. If identity in doubt, check scale and fin ray counts.

Distribution Throughout the Danube catchment.

Habitat Small tributaries and mountain streams.

Feeding Feeds mainly on river bed invertebrates (mayfly and stonefly nymphs, caddis larvae, snails etc.) from dusk onwards. It will take eggs and fry of other fish.

Size Maximum length 20-22cm.

Head fairly broad on top tapering to pointed snout

Eyes high on head

Body scaling extends onto top of head

Small, slightly inferior mouth

First dorsal, tail and pectoral fins are slightly darker than others

Two well-separated dorsal fins; front with VIII–IX spines and rear with 11–13 rays

Dark brown back

Sandy yellow sides with three to four irregular black bands running down at an angle

Long, slender tail terminating in slightly notched tail fin

Scale count: 70–82

Anal fin with I spine + 10–12 rays

Zingel *Zingel (Aspro) zingel*

A slender small relation of the zander, the zingel occurs in Danube and Dniester Rivers. It is a nocturnal species and, like the previous three species, difficult to watch or catch. For certain identification, check scale and fin spine counts.

Distribution The Rivers Danube and Dniester river systems.

Habitat Middle reaches with shallow riffles and deep pools.

Feeding Predominantly invertebrates: mayfly and stonefly nymphs, shrimps, snails. Also tiny fish fry.

Size Most up to 22cm; exceptionally 35–40cm.

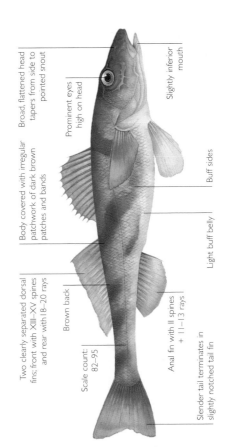

Broad, flattened head tapers from side to pointed snout

Slightly inferior mouth

Prominent eyes high on head

Body covered with irregular patchwork of dark brown patches and bands

Buff sides

Light buff belly

Two clearly separated dorsal fins; front with XIII–XV spines and rear with 18–20 rays

Brown back

Scale count: 82–95

Anal fin with II spines + 11–13 rays

Slender tail terminates in slightly notched tail fin

Thick-lipped Mullet *Chelon labrosus*

This is one of six European species of mullet and although they are primarily marine species, with the thin-lipped (p 180-1), it is most often found in freshwater at the head of estuaries and in brackish creeks. Often big fish, they feed on the tiniest of organic particles.

Distribution Coastal regions from S Norway and Sweden, Ireland and S Britain southwards, including the entire Mediterranean.

Habitat Inshore waters including the heads of estuaries and brackish creeks.

Feeding Shoal fish, feeding on tiny particles of algae and rotting vegetation, microscopic crustaceans, mosquito larvae and landbred flies blown onto the water.

Size Maximum length about 50cm; exceptionally to 75cm weighing up to 4.5kg.

Scales to top of head

Dark grey pectoral fin

Thick-lipped Mullet *Chelon labrosus* 179

Two small, well-separated dorsal fins; front with IV spines and rear with 8–10 rays

Narrow band of fatty material round eyes

Very thick upper lip with three rows of tubercles

Light grey pelvic and anal fins

Grey-blue or green-grey back

White belly

Bright silver or silvery grey sides

Large scales. Scale count: about 45 along sides

Anal fin with II spines + 8–9 rays

Deeply forked, dark grey tail fin

Thin-lipped Mullet *Liza ramada*

A common marine fish that penetrates freshwater in estuaries, thin-lipped mullet sometimes occurs in shoals numbering hundreds, sometimes thousands. It is a particle feeder, enjoying some of the most fetid of food items.

Distribution S Scandinavia and S British Isles southwards to throughout the Mediterranean.

Habitat Inshore waters including estuaries and tidal creeks.

Feeding Any tiny particle of organic matter, including raw sewage and juices of rotting carcasses; also tiny invertebrates.

Size Maximum length 40cm, weight 1.5kg; exceptionally to 2.5kg.

Other similar species Other mullet found in inshore waters, that might be found in brackish estuaries are: golden mullet (*Liza aurata*), sharp-nosed mullet (*L. saliens*), striped mullet (*Mugil cephalus*), and only in the Mediterranean, smooth-lipped mullet (*Oedalechilus labeo*).

Shallowly forked grey tail fin

Large scales over body. Scale count: 44–46 along body

Blue-grey back shading to silver sides with faint grey lines

Anal fin positioned well back on body with III spines + 8–9 rays

Two separated grey dorsal fins; front with IV spines and rear with 8–9 rays

Dark spot at base of pectoral fins

Pelvic and anal fins are lighter grey then other fins

Narrow band of fatty material round eyes

White belly

Very thin upper lip with no tubercles

Broad scaled head, flattened on top

Freshwater Blenny *Blennius fluviatilis*

Blennies are well-known inhabitants of saltwater rock pools around the European coastline, but this species occurs in freshwater in S Europe. They can be watched, resting on boulders with head held high using the pelvic fins, as they watch for potential food.

Distribution S Spain eastwards through Turkey.

Habitat Shallow rivers, lakes and brackish lagoons by the coast.

Feeding Invertebrates from open water (eg crustaceans and pupae) and tiny fish fry.

Size Maximum length 8cm; exceptionally to 15cm.

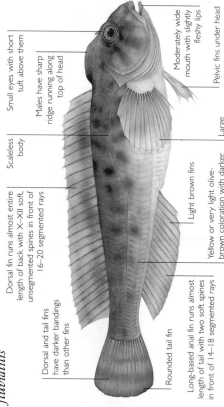

Small eyes with short tuft above them

Males have sharp ridge running along top of head

Moderately wide mouth with slightly fleshy lips

Pelvic fins under head

Scaleless body

Large pectoral fin

Dorsal fin runs almost entire length of back with X–XII soft, unsegmented spines in front of 16–20 segmented rays

Dorsal and tail fins have darker bandings than other fins

Light brown fins

Yellow or very light olive-brown coloration with darker blotches and irregular spots

Rounded tail fin

Long-based anal fin runs almost length of tail with two soft spines in front of 14–18 segmented rays

Common Goby *Pomatoschistus microps*

At least sixteen species of goby might occur in coastal fresh and brackish water, with others found only in the sea. Superficially very similar in structure, all have the pelvic fins held well forward and united to form a sucker, with which the goby can attach on the top of boulders.

Distribution Coastal, from S Norway west around the British Isles S to Gibraltar.

Habitat Marine, plus estuaries and brackish pools.

Feeding Small crustaceans and, in brackish water, midge larvae and pupae; also zooplankton.

Size Average length 5–6cm, exceptionally longer.

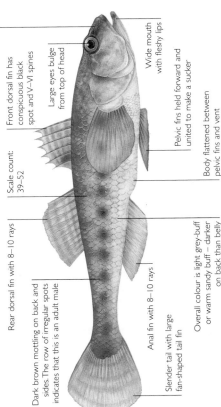

Broad head and blunt snout

Front dorsal fin has conspicuous black spot and V–VI spines

Large eyes bulge from top of head

Wide mouth with fleshy lips

Pelvic fins held forward and united to make a sucker

Body flattened between pelvic fins and vent

Overall colour is light grey-buff or warm sandy buff – darker on back than belly

Anal fin with 8–10 rays

Slender tail with large fan-shaped tail fin

Dark brown mottling on back and sides. The row of irregular spots indicates that this is an adult male

Rear dorsal fin with 8–10 rays

Scale count: 39–52

Mediterranean and Black Sea Gobies

The fifteen gobies listed here are found around Mediterranean and Black Sea coasts and may be found in fresh or brackish water. Close examination is needed to identify a specimen to its species: see *Freshwater Fish* for full details. The classification of these is probably not complete.

Distribution Coastal. Gibraltar and S Spain eastwards and around the Black Sea.

Habitat Shallow inshore waters, and brackish estuaries and brackish lagoons.

Feeding All species feed on invertebrates, including zooplankton, small crustaceans, tiny molluscs and very small fry.

Size Female dwarf gobies reach a maximum length of 2cm, most others 4-6cm, knout goby (Europe's largest) 30-35cm.

Species Canestrini's Goby (*Potamoschistus canestrini*), as shown below, Orsini's Goby (*Knipowitschia punctatissima*), Caucasian Goby (*K. caucasica*), Lesser Black Sea Goby (*K. longecaudata*), Verga's Goby (*K. panizzae*), Pinios Goby (*K. thessala*), Marten's Goby (*Padogobius martensi*), Arno Goby (*P. nigricans*), Monkey Goby (*Neogobius fluviatilis*), Round Goby (*N. melanostomus*), Black Sea Goby (*Proterorhinus marmoratus*), Knout Goby (*Mesogobius batrachocephalus*), Tadpole Goby (*Benthophilus stellatus*), Pygmy Goby (*Economidichthys pygmaeus*), Dwarf Goby (*E. trichonis*).

Large eye on top of head

Thick fleshy lips

Dark brown back

Pelvic fin sucker disk

Belly cream or white

Two separate dorsal fins; front with VI spines and rear with 8–9 rays

Overall coloration is light brown with dark brown markings

All fins cream or sandy with darker markings

Scale count: 36–42

Flounder *Platichthys flesus*

Although the shallow seas around the European continent have several species of flatfish, only the flounder penetrates freshwater, sometimes occurring far upstream in the lower river and in lakes. A popular anglers' fish and culinary species.

Distribution Around almost the entire European coastline from Norway's North Cape southwards through the Mediterranean, but not Iceland.

Habitat Mainly estuarine, but also freshwater rivers and lakes.

Feeding Mainly bottom foods (worms, molluscs, crustaceans) but in estuaries will take shrimps off the bottom.

Size Most attain a maximum length of 30cm, though some reach weights in excess of 1.2kg.

Straight lateral line over most of body, curving upwards slightly close to gill cover

Eyes are usually on right-hand side of body

Eyeless side is white, sometimes with pale buff blotching

Dull grey-brown or dark grey-olive on eyed side, with dull reddish or orange-yellow blotches and darker mottling (fins are similarly marked)

Anal fin with 35–46 rays has sharp, bony spines along base

Dorsal fin with 52–67 rays has sharp, bony spines along base

Scale count: 80–90

Glossary

References in CAPITALS are to other entries in the glossary. Note that fish structures are described on pp 20-1.

Adipose fin A soft fleshy fin located on the back of the fish, behind the DORSAL FIN. It is found, eg in SALMONIDS and black and brown bullheads.

Anal fin The unpaired fin located on the underside of the fish behind the VENT.

Barbel A slender, sensitive 'feeler' found near the mouth of some bottom-feeding fish (eg gudgeons, barbels, European catfish).

Crepuscular Fish active at dusk and dawn.

Cusp A point on a tooth. Important in lamprey identification.

Cyprinid The umbrella name for all members of the carp family (Cyprinidae).

Diurnal Fish that are active by day.

Dorsal fin A fin on the back of the fish that can be double or single.

Feral Fish that are not NATIVE, but have been introduced by man.

Fry Young fish that have recently hatched from eggs.

Gill, gill cover, gill raker The gill cover lies over the gills, which are the fish's respiratory organs. Each gill consists of a bony V-shaped bar with long, red filaments on one side that extract oxygen from the water. On the other side are spiky gill rakers; the structure and number of gill rakers are important in the identification of some species (eg shads).

Hybrid The progeny of a cross between two different species of fish.

Keel, keeled In some species (eg rudd) the sides meet at the belly to produce a sharp ridge or keel.

Larva The immature growing-stage insects.

Lateral line A sensory line running along the sides of the body. Missing or broken in some species.

Native Fish that naturally occur in a river, lake or country.

Nocturnal Fish that are most active at night.

Nymph Immature stage equivalent to LARVA of some insects (eg mayfly and stonefly).

Parr Immature stage of salmon and trout.

Pectoral fins Pair of fins on either side of the body immediately behind the head.

Pelvic fins Paired fins attached to the belly of the fish.

Plankton, zooplankton Microscopic or almost microscopic organisms (zooplankton, animal plankton) that live in open water and drift with strong currents. Plankton includes tiny algae, zooplankton very small crustaceans and the larvae of many other invertebrates.

Pupa A resting stage in the insect life cycle immediately following the LARVA stage.

Salmonid A member of the salmon and trout family (Salmonidae).

Smolt The immature of some SALMONIDS (salmon, sea trout, arctic charr) that heads to sea to feed and grow.

Sucker disc The mouthparts of lampreys.

Tail The body of the fish between the VENT and the base of the TAIL FIN.

Tail fin The fin at the end of the TAIL (sometimes called the Caudal Fin).

Vent The fish anus, normally situated immediately in front of the ANAL FIN.

Index

Page numbers in **bold** refer to
those with illustrations